Authority of

THE EXCELLENT NAME OF JESUS

THE SUPERIOR POWER IN THE NAME OF JESUS

HUMPHREY O. AKPARAH

Dedication

This book is dedicated to my loving children, Chidinma and Eziuche, my motivation and helpers in the ministry; without whom the planting of our first church would have been very difficult.

This is my way of saying thank you to both of you for all the things God has used you to accomplish in Chapel of Success. May God reward you with success, grace, and love in all that you do.

Many thanks to my friend and brother Dr. Charles Osime. Zefe Osime and Azu Okwuobi who provided useful comments, questions, and opinions during the process of editing this book. God bless you all.

Contents

Preface

We see a need in the body of Christ to educate Christians especially young Christians to know, understand, and use the authority that is in the name of Jesus. Young believers need to know from the start the spiritual potentials within them through the name of Jesus. Every believer is equipped to perform miracles, heal sicknesses and diseases, cast out demons, and be baptized in the Holy Ghost whether young or old. These are rights of son-ship in the kingdom of God. The Apostle Peter said, "This promise is to you and your children and to all who are afar off, and as many as the Lord our God will call" (Acts 2:39).

New believers need to understand their rights and privileges as early as possible so they can be useful, fruitful, and steadfast in the things of God. This will prevent them from being tossed about by the diverse winds of destructive doctrines. It will help them to grow faster in their faith in the Lord. They should learn how to live by grace through faith in the name of Jesus. They should be spared the agonies of living a Christian life of defeat, failure, and unprofitable struggles with sin, sicknesses, and pain due to ignorance of who they are and the power they possess in the name of Jesus. The powerful name of Jesus has been given to individual members of the church of Jesus Christ to empower, mature, edify, and safeguard the children of God.

Secondly, this book is an interesting read to mature Christians who may still have some unanswered questions about their faith, rights, and privileges in Christ and to others who want to acquire power for service. The book is as academic as it is spiritual. Any Christian who desires spiritual growth should read and study what is presented in this book. It is written with all Christians in mind, but especially Christians who desire a closer walk with Jesus, and the capacity to perform miracles, signs, and wonders through the name of Jesus Christ.

This book will be a very good teaching and resource tool in the hands of Bible teachers and students in seminaries and Bible schools across the world. The questions and answers in some of the chapters will help to clarify specific issues and questions.

My prayer is that God will use this book to bless you richly. I wish you a very happy reading.

Introduction

This book seeks to help in restoring the power of God to the church to perform miracles, healings, signs, and wonders that Jesus calls us to do. For a long time now the power of God seems to be increasing in the hands of few believers who, by accident or through purposeful seeking, have stumbled onto the secret of that power. This powerful name, JESUS, is given to the body of Christ as a whole and not to just a few privileged ones. The Church of Jesus Christ consists of a body made up of individual believers who should see the power and authority given to them in the name of Jesus manifested in their daily lives through signs, wonders, and miracles. But sadly that is not the case with many Christian believers. I use the words Christian and believer together because there are unbelievers who call themselves Christians.

The church is filled with pastors and believers who tell the stories in the Bible without the demonstration of the power, anointing, and authority that undergirds the living Word of God. If the apostles merely taught the people the story of the power of the name of Jesus, miracles would have completely vanished from Christendom, and Christianity would have lost its power and purpose completely. Thanks be to God who left us records of the Acts of the Apostles and a remnant of the believing ones who still walk and live in the realm of the miraculous through the name of Jesus.

"For the word of God is living and powerful, and sharper than any two-edged sword, piercing even to the division of soul and spirit, and of joints and marrow, and is a discerner of the thoughts and intents of the heart" (Hebrews 4:12-13). Jesus is the Word of God personified. Therefore the name of Jesus is alive, active, and powerful. The name of Jesus is the power of attorney given to the believing, the Church.

It has been the most active force, and the most powerful name in the world since the day Jesus came on scene. The name Jesus is not an ordinary name; it is spirit and has a life giving force within it. It is alive. We should manifest the life and power in the name of Jesus as did the early apostles.

Believers should be taught to see and understand that there is power, actually a superior authority, in that wonder-working name of JESUS. There are other names in the world today that carry authority, but none have as far reaching power and influence as the name of Jesus. Great names come and go and cease to exist the moment the bearer dies, but the name of Jesus lives on, still waxing strong more than two thousand years after He died and rose again.

Jesus is the same yesterday, today, and forever (Hebrews 13:8). It will neither change nor diminish in power. It has not and never will lose any of its authority. However, it appears that believers are losing the revelation of the power and authority in that name.

May I ask you to personally consider the impact of the name of Jesus in your Christian life? Are you increasing in the knowledge of that wonderful name or are you finding it difficult to believe in it for solutions to your problems? Jesus is the solution to all life's problems. Until you believe this truth you might find it difficult to get much result. Absolute faith in Jesus is what God requires from each of us. Pray that God will give you the revelation of that wonder-full, all power-full Name that saved you and washed away your sins when you first believed. However, if you do not know Him as your personal Savior, you can ask Him to come into your heart right now. Please say this short prayer:

"Dear Father in heaven. I come to you in the name of Jesus Christ. I believe that He died for my sins and rose again for my justification. I ask you Lord to forgive my sins and cleanse me from all unrighteousness. I invite Jesus into my heart to be my Lord and personal Savior, and to help me to grow in grace and the knowledge of You. I pray and believe with thanksgiving in the wonderful name of Jesus."

If you are not yet a true believer, you may not have the power and saving grace in this glorious Name. It is not until you believe and fully trust Him that the miracle element in His name will manifest in your life to heal, deliver, and answer prayers today just as it did when Jesus was here physically. Please, patiently read this book to the end and then pass it on and sow it as seed into someone that might need to be awakened to the use of the power in the name of Jesus.

Chapter 1

Superior Authority
In the Name of Jesus

Jesus approached and, breaking the silence, said to them, "All authority (all power of rule) in heaven and on earth has been given to Me. Go then and make disciples of all the nations, baptizing them into the name of the Father and of the Son and of the Holy Spirit, teaching them to observe everything that I have commanded you, and behold, I am with you all the days (perpetually, uniformly, and on every occasion), to the [very] close and consummation of the age."

(Matthew 28:18-20 AMP)

What is a Name?

A name is a word, phrase or sentence by which a person, thing or class of things is called, known or referred to. A name could be descriptive of the quality, character or characteristics, color, odor, position, title, power, reputation, appearance, and nature of the thing or person that bears it. A name is one of the most important attributes of the human nature and existence. Without it there would be chaos in the world. The human mind recognizes the importance of a name, and therefore provides names readily whenever any new thing comes into existence.

In heaven names are even more important. They not only provide the above attributes, some names stand to represent the bearer in heaven, on earth, and underneath the earth. For instance, God's name is said to be "Omnipresent" meaning that it is present in all places at the same time. Therefore, as we survey and dig into the title of this book, may we pay attention to why the name of Jesus is of such a superior nature. It manifests superior power and authority whenever and wherever it is mixed with faith by the believing ones.

How the Name Came About

The name of Jesus came about as a fulfillment of the promises that God made to Adam and Eve in the Garden of Eden (Genesis 3:15) and through prophets like Moses, David, Isaiah, and many others. God spoke through Isaiah to King Ahaz and said, "Therefore the Lord himself shall give you a sign; Behold, a virgin shall conceive, and bear a son, and shall call his name Immanuel" (Isaiah 7:14). Matthew 1:23 says, "Behold, the virgin shall be with child, and bear a Son, and they shall call His name Immanuel, which is translated, 'God with us'." Following this prophecy, Isaiah actually saw the birth of the promised child in the spirit more than 700 years before Emmanuel was actually born and wrote:"For unto us a child is born, unto us a son is given: and the government shall be upon his shoulder: and his name shall be called Wonderful, Counselor, Mighty God, Everlasting Father, Prince of Peace" (Isaiah 9:6).

These prophecies by Isaiah in about 740 B.C. provided some powerful evidence that this child would not be an ordinary child and that His name would not be just an ordinary name. The names we just read above were powerful, heavenly names that have no equal or comparison on earth. Before this child was born, God announced another new name, JESUS. This name was announced to Joseph (the presumptive father of the child) and gave the interpretation of the name as meaning SAVIOR. "And she will bring forth a Son, and you shall call His name Jesus, for He will save His people from their sins" (Matthew 1:21)The Hebrew and Greek root words for savior include: to make safe or safety, freedom, salvation, deliverance, prosperity, liberty, preservation, and rescue.

These prophecies projected even before the child was born that He (His name) was going to be great and special. Jesus came and lived up to the prophecies that went before Him and His name became the saving grace of all mankind. The name of Jesus came as a revelation of God's eternal plan to come down to earth to solve the problems of mankind, and save the world from destruction. Therefore, the name JESUS is the active name of God and is like no other in excellence, power, authority, and grace. The name JESUS = MIRACLE because it brings answers to prayer, healing, deliverance, and much more. As you read, get acquainted with Him, and you will experience life transforming power and miracles in His name.

Powerless Christians

Many Christians have become so powerless that there seems to be no difference between believers and unbelievers. In fact, the atmosphere in some churches is like that of a social club. The messages preached are nothing more than social sermons which do nothing to activate the power in the gospel and in the name of the risen Lord who gave us His name as a legacy.

He [Jesus] said, "And these signs shall follow them that believe; in my name shall they cast out devils; they shall speak with new tongues; They shall take up serpents; and if they drink any deadly poison, it shall not hurt them; they shall lay hands on the sick, and they shall recover. So then after the Lord had spoken unto them, he was received up into heaven, and sat on the right hand of God. And they went forth, and preached every where, the Lord working with them, and confirming the word with signs following."
(Mark16:17-20)

Mark16:17-20)There is power in the name of Jesus. Tremendous power lies hidden within the written word of God (logos). There is also the power of the spoken word (Rhema) which actually carries and manifests the power that is stored in the name of Jesus.

When you use JESUS as just a "word" in preaching or in discussion, you will see none of the power and authority vested in it manifested. But when you use it as the name of God, the name above every other name, and use it with the absolute trust and confidence that signifies that you know and believe Him intimately, then the power of that name is unleashed and comes to bear on the situation for which it is called upon.

JESUS is not an ordinary name like yours and mine. It is a heavenly name vested with the authority of heaven to solve problems on earth—any problem. The name of

Jesus is a problem solver, a life transformer, and a miracle worker. The name is a living being. Jesus lives in His name.

The name Jesus carries within it the integrity of heaven, the integrity of God the Father, the conquests and achievements of Jesus Christ on the cross of Calvary, and the power of the Holy Ghost. "For in Him (Jesus) dwells all the fullness of the Godhead bodily" (Colossians 2:9). That name is the one name that Satan and his demons dread, the only name that sickness and disease bow down to, and the very name that conquered death and the law of gravity. Scripture calls it the Name above every other name.

Therefore God also has highly exalted Him and given Him the name which is above every name, that at the name of Jesus every knee should bow, of those in heaven, and of those on earth, and of those under the earth, and that every tongue should confess that Jesus Christ is Lord, to the glory of God the Father.
(Philippians 2:9-11)

The name of Jesus is a trusted name. It cannot fail. It cannot lose its power. It is too big, too strong, and too "power-full" to fail., I strongly urge and encourage you not to take that name lightly at all, but accord it all the honor and glory and greatness that it deserves. When you begin to do so with all the faith that is in you, then you will begin to see the powers enwrapped in that name unfold before your very eyes.

Beloved, if we know that Jesus is too big to fail why are we so powerless? Why are we afraid to trust Him fully? The problem is not that we do not know that Jesus is bigger than the biggest, higher than the highest, stronger than the strongest, greater than the greatest, wiser than the wisest, and richer than the richest in this world. The problem is that we are insecure in our faith, and therefore we are afraid and lack the absolute confidence required to manifest the power and use the superior authority vested in that name. The problem with Christians today is not the lack of faith, because it does not require "big faith" to use the name of Jesus. It only requires faith as small as a mustard seed.

> *Then came the disciples to Jesus apart, and said, "Why could not we cast him out?" And Jesus said unto them, "Because of your unbelief: for verily I say unto you, If ye have faith as a grain of mustard seed, ye shall say unto this mountain, Remove hence to yonder place; and it shall remove; and nothing shall be impossible unto you."*
>
> (Matthew 17:19-21)

> *Jesus answered and said unto them, "Verily I say unto you, If ye have faith, and doubt not, ye shall not only do this which is done to the fig tree, but also if ye shall say unto this mountain, Be thou removed, and be thou cast into the sea; it shall be done. And all things, whatsoever ye shall ask in prayer, believing, ye shall receive."*
>
> (Matthew 21:21-22)

In Luke 17:5-6 the disciples asked Jesus to increase their faith. "And the apostles said unto the Lord, 'Increase our faith.' And the Lord said, 'If ye had faith as a grain of mustard seed, ye might say unto this sycamine tree, Be thou plucked up by the root, and be thou planted in the sea; and it should obey you'."

I believe Jesus told them that their problem at that point

was not the absence or lack of a big faith, but of not being able to use the faith they already possessed with confidence and without doubting. Every believer has been given a measure of (spiriitual) faith from the time they were born again, and it continues to grow as they mature in the Lord. But most people do not believe that they have enough faith to do great things in the name of Jesus, for the kingdom of God and even for themselves.

Jesus was simply telling the disciples to use the small faith they had because their faith, even if it was as small as a mustard seed, could accomplish great things. In other words, Jesus was reminding them that they already had enough faith to move mountains. Beloved, your small faith can accomplish great things in the kingdom of God if you will put it to work. If you can believe and not doubt the Word or your own faith, there is still tremendous power in the name of Jesus.

It is not our power that will do the job that needs to be done. It is God who does it through us. "For it is God who works in you both to will and to do for His good pleasure"(Philippians 2:13). God wants to use us to do His work. It is not us using God to do His work. It is Jesus working in us and through us, in partnership with us to meet our needs and solve our problems. Working with Jesus is not as hard as it seems. The name of Jesus is so powerful and so self-sustaining that it will accomplish whatever we trust Him to do for us. It does not require big faith to use the name of Jesus. It takes just a small confident trust, a settled assurance, and an undoubting and unwavering belief in the big name of JESUS.

Years ago when I was conducting deliverance ministrations, God taught me that I didn't need to stress myself out trying to cast out demons in people. He showed me how to get the demons out by a simple command through the person that was oppressed. Then I would lead the person in a simple prayer of faith, and before you know it the oppressed person was completely set free. From then on I started to see miracles of healing, deliverance, answers to prayer, and people baptized in the Holy Ghost.

Too Big to Fail

The name JESUS is too big to fail because back of it is the omnipotence, omnipresence, and omniscience of the Most High. It is covered by the powers of heaven and the divine integrity of the Almighty. The name Jesus is a tasted, tried, and proven authority in heaven, on earth, and in the dark regions of Satan's domain. Even death could not defeat or hold Him captive. Therefore, our small problems are nothing to Him if we bring them to Him in the right way.

> *Men of Israel, hear these words: Jesus of Nazareth, a Man attested by God to you by miracles, wonders, and signs which God did through Him in your midst, as you yourselves also know... whom God raised up, having loosed the pains of death, because it was not possible that He should be held by it.*
> (Acts 2:22, 24)

The name Jesus commands and controls the inexhaustible resources of heaven. It also controls the hearts and souls of all men on earth. His name is stronger than and more solid rock or fortress. . There is absolutely nothing in the universe equal to, comparable to or that can make that Name fail. Jesus Christ, the man that bears that name, is right now sitting in the highest position in the universe, far above every other name, title, and position ever known to man or the angels. Yet that name is very near and very present to those who believe in Him, and call on His name out of a pure and sincere heart of faith and obedience.

And the devil said unto him, If thou be the Son of God, command this stone that it be made bread. And Jesus answered him, saying, It is written, That man shall not live by bread alone, but by every word of God.

And the devil, taking him up into an high mountain, shewed unto him all the kingdoms of the world in a moment of time. And the devil said unto him, All this power will I give thee, and the glory of them: for that is delivered unto me; and to whomsoever I will I give it. If thou therefore wilt worship me, all shall be yours. And Jesus answered and said unto him, Get thee behind me, Satan: for it is written, Thou shalt worship the Lord thy God, and him only shalt thou serve.

And he brought him to Jerusalem, and set him on a pinnacle of the temple, and said unto him, If thou be the Son of God, cast thyself down from there: For it is written, He shall give his angels charge over thee, to keep thee: And in their hands they shall bear thee up, lest at any time thou dash thy foot against a stone. And Jesus answering said unto him, It is said, Thou shalt not tempt the Lord thy God. And when the devil had ended all the temptation, he departed from him for a season.

(Luke 4:3-13)

Satan tried to trick Jesus, but he departed in shame and ignominy because Jesus was too big for him and too strong to fall by the tricks of Satan. If Satan could not trick Him to fall nothing else can. If the fear of death and the weight of the sins of whole world on His shoulder did not intimidate Him to falter, nothing else can. When Jesus arose from the grave He said, "All power (authority) is given to me in heaven and earth" (Matthew 28:18). Satan and all the host of his demons know that the name Jesus is too big, too powerful, and too holy to fail.

We, the believing ones, should not be afraid to call on that name with full confidence and assurance, because Jesus bequeathed it to us as an inheritance. If we know that God cannot allow the name of Jesus to fail without seeing Himself fail, let us then come boldly with complete assurance and trust in His faithfulness to back up His word and His promises. Jesus is the name of the Son of God, the second person in the trinity, the man of Galilee, and He is alive on the planet earth today and will be for all eternity.

Jesus, being God in His own right, cannot fail without dragging down the Father and the Holy Spirit with Him. This is impossible and absolutely preposterous even to think of. Even if heaven and earth would fall to pieces, the Word of God and the name of Jesus cannot fail. Jesus is that Word of God so it cannot and will not fail you. You can bet on it, trust it, rely on it, and absolutely depend on it to carry you, support you, secure you, heal you, and sustain you. The name Jesus will never disappoint. If you've been disappointed, it is not the name. It may be your fear or doubt or insecurity that failed. The name Jesus is too holy and righteous to lie, and simply too big to fail. It carries within it the nature and essence of invincibility and indestructibility.

Chapter 2

The Secret of Power

One thing everybody is very desirous of is the secret of the power of Jesus as demonstrated by the early disciples. In fact some have paid money in order to acquire this secret. Some have gone to Bible schools, others have fasted upward of forty days, but most have failed to find the secret. In the Acts of the Apostles, one man named Simon saw the miracles that the apostles performed. He also saw that through the laying on of the apostles' hands the people received the Holy Ghost. He offered them money to receive this power.

And when Simon saw that through laying on of the apostles' hands the Holy Ghost was given, he offered them money, Saying, Give me also this power, that on whomsoever I lay hands, he may receive the Holy Ghost. But Peter said unto him, Thy money perish with thee, because thou hast thought that the gift of God may be purchased with money. Thou hast neither part nor lot in this matter: for thy heart is not right in the sight of God.

(Acts 8:18-21)

Is there a secret or mystery to receiving and using the power of God? Can an "ordinary" Christian receive this power or is it meant for an exclusive few? Is there a price to be paid and if so what is it? Why are so many without the power the early church demonstrated?

Yes, there is a mystery to the power in the name of Jesus. If there was no mystery everybody would have found it and used it to solve their problems. The sad thing is most people are looking in the wrong places, doing the wrong things or are not searching long enough. Jeremiah 29:13 says, "And you shall seek Me and find Me when you shall search with your whole heart."

The good news is that the mystery of the power in the superior name of Jesus is not meant for a chosen few. It is freely given to those who seek earnestly for it. Psalm 25:14 says, "The secret of the LORD is with them that fear (love) him; and he will shew them his covenant."God is always very interested in the people that love Him and fear Him. He wants to give them the best of every spiritual gift. Peter did not start performing miracles until Jesus got from him an unequivocal, unconditional confession of Peter's love for Him. In John 21:15-19 Jesus confronted Peter with these soul searching questions.

So when they had eaten breakfast, Jesus said to Simon Peter, "Simon, son of Jonah, do you love Me more than these?" He said to Him, "Yes, Lord; You know that I love You." He said to him, "Feed My lambs." He said to him again a second time, "Simon, son of Jonah, do you love Me?" He said to Him, "Yes, Lord; You know that I love You." He said to him, "Tend My sheep." He said to him the third time, "Simon, son of Jonah, do you love Me?" Peter was grieved because

He said to him the third time, "Do you love Me?" And he said to Him, "Lord, You know all things; You know that I love You." Jesus said to him, "Feed My sheep. Most assuredly, I say to you, when you were younger, you girded yourself and walked where you wished; but when you are old, you will stretch out your hands, and another will gird you and carry you where you do not wish." This He spoke, signifying by what death he would glorify God. And when He had spoken this, He said to him, "Follow Me."

God does not give His power haphazardlyHis power is for the glorification of His Son Jesus and not for selfish purposes The man named Simon in the Acts of the Apostles wanted to buy and use the power for purposes other than to glorify God and His Son. He wanted to use it as a money-making business. He was already a sorcerer. He wanted to combine the power of Satan and the power of God to make more money.

Another example of the selfish intention for the use of the power of God was found with the disciples of Jesus themselves. In Luke 9:54-56 we read, "And when his disciples James and John saw this, they said, Lord, wilt thou that we command fire to come down from heaven, and consume them, even as Elias did? But he (Jesus) turned, and rebuked them, and said, Ye know not what manner of spirit ye are of. For the Son of man is not come to destroy men's lives, but to save them."

Jesus did not die to perpetrate our selfishness but to save us from it. Therefore, He would not invest His power, His secret to those who would use it to their selfish ends or add foolishness to selfishness. God's power is for those who love Him and love their neighbors as themselves.

How Can This Mystery Be Solved?

The secret of power is a mystery and mysteries can only be interpreted by revelations. One who does not have the revelation of who Jesus Christ is can not receive the mystery of His name or mystery of His power. The point I am making here is not about being born again. Anybody can be born again, but not all can use the secret of His power. It comes by the revelation of the living Word to a willing heart.

The Word of God is the beginning and end of that mystery. The knowledge of this secret cannot be acquired other than from the Word of God. It is a secret because it is not written in one place, it is scattered all over the Bible. One must do a diligent search to see and receive the revelation. Someone asked me, "Does this mean that the power in the name of Jesus is a mystery?"

My answer is it is a mystery because it produces miracles, and we know that miracles are direct divine interventions of God in the affairs of men. It is beyond human comprehension and explanation. You only have to believe it to experience it. Granted, some may stumble upon this revelation or power by accident, others receive it as a gift, but most people find it by deliberate, even desperate seeking, searching, and revelation.

In Matthew 6:33 Jesus said, "But seek first the kingdom of God and His righteousness, and all these things shall be added to you." In Jeremiah 29:13 God said, "And you will seek Me and find Me, when you search for Me with all your heart." The Psalmist prayed, "Open thou mine eyes that I may behold wondrous (wonder-full) things out of thy law (Word)" (Psalm 119:18).

Indeed there are wonders and wonderful things in the Word of God. There are unsearchable, inexhaustible riches, power, and blessing hidden in the Word of God. Only a few people have tapped into the vast ocean of the power and rich resources stored up in His Word. It takes revelation knowledge of the Word, and the divine insight that comes from a thirsty heart to find these hidden secrets. Peter, Paul, Philip, and others had very close, very personal encounters with Jesus. Down through the years since the Man of Miracles left this world, all those who have moved in the supernatural anointing of God have been men and woman who have had a personal encounter and revelation of the Son of God.

Jesus must reveal this personally for you to have the kind of relationship whereby He can entrust to your care His very essence, the power that makes Him God. It is sharing in His divine nature as spoken of in 2 Peter 1:3-4. Receiving the secret of power is receiving a part of God's divine nature.

As His divine power has given to us all things that pertain to life and godliness, through the knowledge of Him who called us by glory and virtue, by which have been given to us exceedingly great and precious promises, that through these you may be partakers of the divine nature, having escaped the corruption that is in the world through lust.

Receiving the secret of power is sharing in the mystery of the divinity of God. Therefore, God must be sure that you love Him, and will use the power He will entrust to you for its intended purposes. For this reason, even people who received the authority in the name of Jesus stand to lose it if they begin to work in pride, unrighteousness, and sin.Another question I received in the course of writing this book was, "Can an individual seek God's revelation? If so, how?"

Again my answer is found within the Word of God. There are only a few places in Scripture that God gave group revelations. Most revelations were given to individuals who diligently sought God. Seeking God to receive power is usually a personal affair. It is a process that involves much prayer and fasting. Such prayers are usually done in your closet and not in prayer meetings.

A follow up question asked by this same person was, "Is the manifestation of the power in the name of Jesus through miracles a sure sign of the revelation?"

I would say that to a large extent it is, but not completely. There are other ways an individual can receive the revelation of the power of God. It all depends on what you are seeking or asking God for. Performing miracles and healings are just a few of the many gifts of God to the church; there are many others. Read 1 Corinthians 12:1-11 for further study on this.

God is a revelator. He can and does reveal secrets to those who seek for them. There must be a hunger and thirst for the relationship that produces the living water of God. John 7:37-39 says, "On the last day, that great day of the feast, Jesus stood and cried saying, 'If any man thirst, let him come unto me, and drink. He that believeth on me, as the scripture hath said, out of his belly shall flow rivers of living water. (But this spake he of the Spirit, which they that believe on him should receive: for the Holy Ghost was not yet given; because that Jesus was not yet glorified.)'"Revelations come through the Holy Spirit.

It is not that God has made it difficult for people to find out the secret of His power, rather it is because God's people have other priorities, goals, ambitions, and interests that they place above the knowledge of God. These priorities hinder deep spiritual hunger. Even though man earnestly desires the power and anointing of God, he prefers to attend to the cares and pleasures of this world rather than to seek first the kingdom of God and His righteous power.

The requirement for receiving the power is to intentionally seek the kingdom of God and His righteousness. We must not even allow our call to the ministry push our relationship with God to a secondary position. God is spirit and all those who seek Him for power must do so in spirit and in truth (John 4:24). If believers and ministers were to devote more of their time and energies in seeking and searching for the power of God, the church would not be as powerless as it is now. We need to repent before God, and reorganize our priorities if we are to move in the divine power of God.

The Secret of Power Is the Word

The Word of God is sacred and is anointed with power. It is a living thing. The Word of God is God. He watches over His Word to see that it is fulfilled. "The Lord said to me," says Jeremiah 1:12, "You have seen correctly, for I am watching to see that my word is fulfilled" (NIV). Jesus said, "It is the Spirit who gives life; the flesh profits nothing. The words that I speak to you are spirit, and they are life" (John 6:63).

In other words, the Word of God is a living thing and carries within it the spirit and power of God. God also said He has magnified His Word, Jesus, above every other thing in heaven and on earth. We can trust the Word and the Name to save a sinner, heal a sick person, raise the dead, and meet our needs. The Psalmist said, "I will bow down toward your holy temple and will praise your name for your love and your faithfulness, for you have exalted above all things your name and your word" (Psalm 138:2 NIV). Another translation renders the second part as,"…for You have magnified Your word above all Your name" (NKJV). The secret of power is the Word of God. God's Word is energized with power, therefore, God has magnified His Word above everything else. There can be nothing greater to the child of God who is seeking to receive the power of God than the Word and the name of Jesus. Knowledge of God is not an academic thing. It is not received through reading books alone. Books are good and what you read is what you know and manifest. What you read all day is what you think of all day. As a man thinks in his heart so he is (Proverbs 23:7).

The knowledge of God's power is a spiritual knowledge and using the name of Jesus is faith based. Heart and not head knowledge of the Word of God is indispensable to receiving the truth of the secret of the power that is in the name of Jesus. The Apostle Paul wrote in2 Timothy 2:15, "Study to shew thyself approved unto God, a workman that needeth not to be ashamed, rightly dividing the word of truth." Studying the Word to know God intimately is different from studying just to teach or preach. The former focuses on you and God, but the later focuses on you and your audience. The two are not the same at all.

To know Jesus the healer you must study the healing ministry of Jesus. To know Jesus the miracle worker you must study the miracles of Jesus. To receive power you must study the Word that deals with the demonstration of the power of God in the Scriptures. You must focus on a God-centered study and not an academic or audience-centered one. It is in so doing that you will receive the knowledge and the Spirit that will guide you to focus your prayers correctly. After the study comes the courting of God's favor and friendship. This is another dimension of knowing God.

There is tremendous power in the Word of God. All the power we need has already been released into the Word. When we discover and apply or act on the Word of God, power is manifested, miracles happen, and God is glorified in the Son—Jesus.

Chapter 3

Power Released Preaching the Word

The power of God is release in the name of Jesus through the preaching of the Word of God in order to bring glory to God. In no other way can you experience a mighty release of the power than through preaching the kingdom of God.

> *Then Philip went down to the city of Samaria, and preached Christ unto them. And the people with one accord gave heed unto those things which Philip spake, hearing and seeing the miracles which he did. For unclean spirits, crying with loud voices, came out of many that were possessed with them: and many taken with palsies, and that were lame, were healed. And there was great joy in that city. But when they believed Philip preaching the things concerning the kingdom of God, and the name of Jesus Christ, they were baptized, both men and women.*
>
> (Acts 8:5-8, 12)

Power is released for and in the preaching of the gospel of Jesus Christ. For that reason, everyone who believes can receive the power of God. It is not preserved for a few blessed or favored people. God is no respecter of persons. All can have it. Everyone is invited. Revelation 22:17 says, "And the Spirit and the bride say, Come. And let him that heareth say, Come. And let him that is athirst come. And whosoever will, let him take the water of life freely." Power comes through practical application of the Word of God. Power in the name of Jesus is demonstrated in preaching, personal evangelism, mass evangelism, Bible studies, church services, and all other such gatherings in the name of Jesus for the sole purpose of advancing the kingdom of God and glorifying the Father through the Son. This power is the power of heaven, and must be used for heaven's purposes.

These Signs Shall Follow Them That Believe

Jesus made a startling pronouncement, perhaps one of the greatest words that ever fell out of the lips of the miracle worker Himself in Mark 16:17-10. The Man in whose name resides the superior authority is the subject of Mark's Gospel. These were His very last words and are worthy of our undivided and conscious attention.

"And these signs shall follow them that believe; In my name shall they cast out devils; they shall speak with new tongues; They shall take up serpents; and if they drink any deadly poison, it shall not hurt them; they shall lay hands on the sick, and they shall recover. So then after the Lord had spoken unto them, he was received up into heaven, and sat on the right hand

*of God. And they went forth, and preached every
where, the Lord working with them, and confirming
the word with signs following."*

When Jesus made those pronouncements, the disciples
did not understand all that He was talking about, just as you
might not understand all that I am saying until you do what
the disciples did after Jesus was taken up. What did they
do that turned them into miracle-working machines like
their ascended master? Mark 16:20 answers this question
for us. "And they went forth, and preached every where,
the Lord working with them, and confirming the word with
signs following." This is perhaps the most difficult of all the
requirements for a continued flow of power in the church
today. Preaching and speaking the Word almost always pre-
cedes large scale miracles.

Have you ever wondered why, after all your studying
and believing, you see little or no miracles? It could be
that you are missing out on the command to go and preach
the gospel. "And he said unto him or her, Go ye into all
the world, and preach the gospel to every creature" (Mark
16:15). May God give us a revelation of the power that is
released during the preaching of the gospel.

If you want to see these signs, begin immediately to
put the principles enunciated in this book into practice. If
you want to see the power of God manifested in your life
and in your church, practice praying for the sick or any
other problems people have when you go out to evange-
lize. If you want to see the kingdom of God on earth as it
is in heaven, begin to go everywhere with the gospel. You
will begin to see a tremendous move of the power of God
in your life and ministry. Is this command for preachers
alone? No, it is for all Christians. However, you must be a

believer in miracles. If you don't believe you will not have the confidence to ask for it. Miracles can happen to anyone, but especially to those who ask and are expecting or anticipating it. The power in the name of Jesus responds readily to the preaching of the kingdom message. God wants to hear us preach and talk about His kingdom here on earth. He wants to bring His kingdom to earth as soon and as fast as possible.

For that reason, when Jesus was teaching His disciple how to pray He said in Matthew 6:9-10, "After this manner therefore pray ye: Our Father which art in heaven, Hallowed be thy name. Thy kingdom come, Thy will be done in earth, as it is in heaven." It is God's heart desire to bring His kingdom down to earth. He is being delayed because believers have not gotten the revelation that God is waiting to come down to permanently be with us and set up His kingdom here on the earth. When He sent His only begotten Son to this world He called His name Emmanuel, meaning God with us.

The Son said to His disciples, "Ye have heard how I said unto you, I go away, and come again unto you. If ye loved me, ye would rejoice, because I said, I go unto the Father: for my Father is greater than I" (John14:28)Until the believer receives this revelation and begins to pray for God's kingdom to come quickly, and begins to live in urgent expectation, the delay will continue. It is time we begin to see an outrageous manifestation and outpouring of the Spirit for miracles in our churches, in our lives, and in our world.

There is already this great expectation in heaven among the angels and the inhabitants of the celestial kingdoms. Take a look at what is already happening and will continue to happen until the ultimate fulfillment of this prophecy.

"And the seventh angel sounded; and there were great voices in heaven, saying, The kingdoms of this world are become the kingdoms of our Lord, and of his Christ; and he shall reign for ever and ever. And the four and twenty elders, which sat before God on their seats, fell upon their faces, and worshipped God, Saying, We give thee thanks, O LORD God Almighty, which art, and wast, and art to come; because thou hast taken to thee thy great power, and hast reigned" (Luke 4:3-1).God wants to give you the power of His kingdom. He wants you to enjoy the manifestation of His power here on earth with all the blessings and privileges that go with it. Jesus prayed, "Thine is the Kingdom the Power and the glory forever and ever. Amen." The power for miracles is the power of the Father in the Son and through the Holy Ghost. After Jesus arose from the dead, He came and spoke to them saying, "All power is given unto me in heaven and in earth. Go ye therefore, and teach all nations, baptizing them in the name of the Father, and of the Son, and of the Holy Ghost: Teaching them to observe all things whatsoever I have commanded you: and, lo, I am with you always, even unto the end of the world. Amen" (Matthew 28:18-20).

Jesus sends us to go and herald the kingdom of God. He promised that He would go with us in the power of His name. So let us go, child of God, for He will not fail us. He is too big to fail. He is ever faithful. Heaven and earth could pass away but the faithfulness of God will not pass from you.

Obedience

Obedience to the Word of God is the only key to success in life and in ministry. It is the key to witnessing the demonstration of the power of the gospel. When I say obedience I mean total, complete, full, and unconditional obedience to what the Word says. This is a thorny issue. What constitutes total obedience? How do I know that I am obeying God fully? Can anybody truly obey God completely? These and more questions are what may be going through your mind now as you read this important information.

Obedience is in the heart. True obedience is measured by the peace and joy that accompanies a particular action or inaction that you take in compliance to a directive or law of God. God interprets His written Word in our spirits so we can understand it and obey it. If there is any confusion or doubt concerning an action or if we are not experiencing peace of mind regarding God's Word, it might mean that action is not in complete obedience. The Bible says, "Whatever is not of faith is sin" (Romans 14:23).

Partial obedience is sometimes worse than no obedience at all because it leaves us with a sense of accomplishment or false hope before God. God expects us to obey Him fully. An example of partial obedience in the Bible concerns the case of Saul, king of Israel. God sent Saul to completely destroy a city called Amalek and everything in it: men, women, children, sheep, goats, oxen, and then burn the city with fire (1 Samuel 15).

Saul actually went and fought with Amalekites and destroyed the city, but he and his soldiers took some of the sheep, oxen, and other valuables. Saul also brought back Agag, the king of Amalek. That partial obedience angered God so much that He regretted setting up Saul as king of Israel. Samuel the prophet made this famous declaration concerning the sin of partial obedience in 1 Samuel 15:22-23.

"Has the Lord as great delight in burnt offerings and sacrifices, as in obeying the voice of the Lord? Behold, to obey is better than sacrifice, And to heed than the fat of rams. For rebellion is as the sin of witchcraft, And stubbornness is as iniquity and idolatry. Because you have rejected the word of the Lord, He also has rejected you from being king."

Every disobedience is sin and partial obedience is also sin. We see another example in Acts 5:1-11 concerning Ananias and Sapphira who sold their land and brought part of the money to the apostles. Apparently God had told them to give the whole amount to the church, but they decided not to obey God fully. They took out a portion and brought the rest to the apostles. God's anger was kindled against them and they died instantly, one after the other for lying.

Thank God for the spirit of grace in this dispensation. How many of us have done such things or worse and have gotten away with it? How many of us live our lives in partial obedience to God? However, when it comes to the release of power, God requires full obedience even now in this time of grace. When we seek to obey God fully He grants us the enablement, the grace, and the power to do His will. As I write this book I am reminded that I need to repent in the area of partial obedience.

Obedience is an act of faith in God's Word. It is our spiritual worship. It is placing our implicit confidence in our Lord. When we do, God is honored and glorified in His Son our Redeemer and we receive our petitions. No one can see God with the human eyes, therefore, trusting the Word of God and obeying it is the only way to trust and obey God.

Legacy

The name of Jesus is bequeathed to us, the church, as a legacy by our ascended Lord. A legacy is an inheritance of worth, a gift of value, and a birthright blessing handed down from our ancestry. The name of Jesus is given to the church and to the individual members of the body of Christ with all the powers, authority, rights, privileges, and conquests that pertain to it. Jesus said, "I will not leave you as orphans" (John 14:18). He did not leave the disciples or the church with no hope or inheritance. He bequeathed to us His name, an ever-increasing and renewable inheritance. The Bible says, "The name of the Lord is a strong tower the righteous run into it and are safe" (Proverbs 18:10).

Jesus kept His promise to send His disciples His Holy Spirit to enable them to carry on His work. Using the power in His name, His disciples witnessed miracles, signs, and wonders. From that time on things began to happen wherever they went. The lame walked, the dead were raised, the sick were healed, and the Lord did many more signs and wonders through them to confirm that He was indeed with them.

Jesus is the same today as He was then. That name has lost none of its power. Not only did He give us His name, He gave us the authority to represent Him as His ambassadors and to use His name on His behalf, so that "whatever we bind on earth shall be bound in heaven and what ever we loose on earth shall be loosed in heaven" (Matthew 16:19).

Now then, we are ambassadors for Christ, as though God were pleading through us: we implore you on Christ's behalf, be reconciled to God.

(2 Corinthians 5:20)

We have been appointed and credentialed to represent Jesus in this world through the Holy Spirit we received when we believed. We have been given power and authority to bless, bind and loose, heal, cast out demons, and proclaim the kingdom of our God here on earth. That statement from Paul in 2 Corinthians 5:20 has turned us into the Lord's personal ambassador plenipotentiaries. That statement is so profound that if we understand the full impact of it, we will be as bold as lions and as strong and unmovable as solid rocks.

Jesus gave us the right to use His name in our prayers and in our gatherings, and He promised that He will be there among us when we do. "For where two or three are gathered together in My name, I am there in the midst of them" (Matthew 18:20). He also promisedthat He will answer us when we ask anything in His name. "And whatsoever ye shall ask in my name, that will I do, that the Father may be glorified in the Son. If ye shall ask any thing in my name, I will do it" (John 14:13-14).   This passage suggests that when we pray or use the name of Jesus to ask anything that we desire from God the Father, Jesus Himself promises to answer it. For example, if I have a headache or I have some bills to pay and I ask God to heal me or help me pay my bill, Jesus said He will answer my prayer. What He did not say, though, is when or how He will do it. Jesus does not bind Himself to human timing. I believe that He was saying He will make sure that it is done, that it will be taken care of, and that I will get my bill paid for sure. God is never late. It will be taken care of on time, God's time. This passage also means that the moment we pray or ask in Jesus' name, He immediately assumes the responsibility to see that our prayer is answered. We do need to read the whole promise however, because it also says that the prayer must be according to the will of God. "Now this is the confidence that we have in Him, that if we ask anything according to His will, He hears us. And if we know that He hears us, whatever we ask, we know that we have our petitions that we asked of Him" (1 John 5:14-15). We need not continue to worry once we pray. If anybody should worry, it should be Jesus who promised and gave us His word of honor. He would take care of it. Whenever we pray in Jesus name we put His reputation on the line. For that reason we can count on Him. He cannot fail because God values His integrity. He knows that the more He answers our prayers, the more we will pray, and the more glory He will get. This is a win-win situation for us and the Godhead. Another outstandingly and memorable promise made by Jesus is found in John 16: 24. "Until now you have asked nothing in My name. Ask, and you will receive, that your joy may be full." All thewhile Jesus was physically in the world with His disciples, they had prayed as the Jews did only to the Father. But shortly before He died and rose again, Jesus taught them to pray or ask through His name. He made the above declaration and commanded them to begin to ask for all their needs and to receive the answers through His name so that they will have a full and complete joy. The above statement is a promise. It is a legal authorization. It is a power of attorney. You better take it seriously. You can hold Him to His Word. Jesus is saying the same thing to us today. He wants us to be happy, joyful, and blessed when we call on His name. He want us to know that He has put His reputation and the power of His name on the line for us so that we will be happy serving Him. It was never God's intention to leave us alone as believers. He is with us in the power and authority of His name. We know that there is superior authority in the superior name of Jesus.

Beloved, have faith in God and put your whole trust in the name of Jesus when you pray because it is backed up by heaven and all its resources. It will never fail you. It is the highest name ever mentioned in this world and there will never be any other name like it. Jesus is the active name of the One and Only True and Living God.

Chapter 4

What Does the Name Jesus Mean to You?

In the light of the foregoing, what does the name of Jesus mean to you? How have you related to that name in the past and how will you relate to it now and in the future? Have you yet received the revelation of that name or do you need more proof? Jesus, as a name and as a person, is recognized in heaven, on earth, and under the earth. Have you personally recognized and accepted Him as your Lord and Savior? The prophets of old did, astrologers did, the disciples did, demons did and still do, and Satan did and still does, too. Above all, God the Father Almighty always does.

We shall examine what each of the individuals above had to say about the man Jesus. First, let us see what the prophets said about Him. The prophets were the first to recognize Jesus in the spirit more than 700 years before Christ was born. The first of them was Moses, the man that led the children of Israel out of Egypt.

Moses

Moses saw Jesus as a prophet, and a great and mighty deliverer like himself. "The Lord your God will raise up for you a Prophet like me from your midst, from your brethren. Him you shall hear" (Deuteronomy18:15). This prophecy was fulfilled in Jesus Christ. The Apostle Peter explained it to the Jews that Jesus was the fulfillment of that prophecy in Acts 7:37-38. "This is that Moses who said to the children of Israel, 'The Lord your God will raise up for you a Prophet like me from your brethren. Him you shall hear.' This is he who was in the congregation in the wilderness with the Angel who spoke to him on Mount Sinai, and with our fathers, the one who received the living oracles to give to us."**Isaiah**

Isaiah the prophetsaw and recognized Jesus and wrote . "For unto us a Child is born, unto us a Son is given; and the government will be upon His shoulder. And His name will be called Wonderful, Counselor, Mighty God, Everlasting Father, Prince of Peace" (Isaiah 9:6). Isaiah even prophesied of His virgin birth. "Therefore the Lord Himself will give you a sign: Behold, the virgin shall conceive and bear a Son, and shall call His name Immanuel" (Isaiah 7:14).

John the Baptist

In the Gospel of John, we see the last of the Old Testament prophets, John the Baptist. When he saw Jesus for the first time he declared, "Behold the Lamb of God that takes away the sin of the world" (John 1:29). John was the first man to recognize that Jesus was Lamb of God.

The Disciples of Jesus

The disciples of Jesus had this to say about their master when He wanted to know if they recognized who He was.

When Jesus came into the region of Caesarea Philippi, He asked His disciples, saying, "Who do men say that I, the Son of Man, am?" So they said, "Some say John the Baptist, some Elijah, and others Jeremiah or one of the prophets." He said to them, "But who do you say that I am? Simon Peter answered and said, "You are the Christ, the Son of the living God." Jesus answered and said to him, "Blessed are you, Simon Bar-Jonah, for flesh and blood has not revealed this to you, but My Father who is in heaven.

(Matthew 16:13-17; John 6:68)

A Centurion Recognized Jesus

The centurion among the Roman soldiers who tortured and crucified Jesus recognized Him as truly the son of God. "So when the centurion and those with him, who were guarding Jesus, saw the earthquake and the things that had happened, they feared greatly, saying, 'Truly this was the Son of God'" (Matthew 27:54).

Thomas

Thomas was one of the disciples of Jesus who was absent when Jesus visited the disciples the first time after His resurrection. When Thomas came back and was told that Jesus had risen indeed and had appeared to them, he did not believe them. When Jesus appeared the second time when Thomas was with the rest, Jesus showed His nail scars to Thomas then Thomas recognized Jesus as God and received Him as his Lord.

And after eight days His disciples were again inside, and Thomas with them. Jesus came, the doors being shut, and stood in the midst, and said, "Peace to you!" Then He said to Thomas, "Reach your finger here, and look at My hands; and reach your hand here, and put it into My side. Do not be unbelieving, but believing. And Thomas answered and said to Him, "My Lord and my God."

(John 20:26-28)

Demons

The truth that Jesus was the Son of God was well known to Satan and his host of demons. Whenever they encountered Jesus face-to-face, they proclaimed that they knew and recognized Him"Now in the synagogue there was a man who had a spirit of an unclean demon. And he cried out with a loud voice, saying, 'Let us alone! What have we to do with You, Jesus of Nazareth? Did You come to destroy us? I know who You are—the Holy One of God!'" (Luke 4:33-34).

We see this trend repeated in all the gospels. In Matthew 8:28-29, we see another encounter. "When He had come to the other side, to the country of the Gergesenes there met Him two demon-possessed men, coming out of the tombs, exceedingly fierce, so that no one could pass that way. And suddenly they cried out, saying, 'What have we to do with You, Jesus, You Son of God? Have You come here to torment us before the time?'."

Satan

Immediately after Jesus ended His forty days of fasting in the wilderness, the devil came and tempted Him by appealing to Jesus' hunger and sense of pride as the Son of God.

If You are the Son of God command that these stones become bread. But He answered and said, It is written, Man shall not live by bread alone, but by every word that proceeds from the mouth of God.

(Matthew 4:3-4)

This time in the wilderness was the only recorded close encounter that Jesus had with Satan during His earthly ministry. Satan obviously knew who Jesus was and tried to derail His ' ministry before it even got started.

Angels

Before His birth the angels announced to Joseph and Mary that a holy child would be born to them. After His birth the angels heralded His arrival!

Then the angel said to her, "Do not be afraid, Mary, for you have found favor with God. And behold, you will conceive in your womb and bring forth a Son, and shall call His name Jesus. He will be great, and will be called the Son of the Highest; and the Lord God will give Him the throne of His father David. And He will reign over the house of Jacob forever, and of His kingdom there will be no end." Then Mary said to the angel, "How can this be, since I do not know a man?" And the angel answered and said to her, "The Holy Spirit will come upon you, and the power of the Highest will overshadow you; therefore, also, that Holy One who is to be born will be called the Son of God.

(Luke 1:30-35)

Now there were in the same country shepherds living out in the fields, keeping watch over their flock by night. And behold an angel of the Lord stood before them, and the glory of the Lord shone around them, and they were greatly afraid. Then the angel said to them, "Do not be afraid, for behold, I bring you good tidings of great joy which will be to all people. For there is born to you this day in the city of David a Savior, who is Christ the Lord. And this will be the sign to you: You will find a Babe wrapped in swaddling cloths, lying in a manger." And suddenly there was with the angel a multitude of the heavenly host praising God and saying: Glory to God in the highest, and on earth peace, goodwill toward men!"

(Luke 2:8-14)

God the Father

The Father spoke a number of times to announce His Son Jesus and to authenticate Jesus' Son-ship. The first was immediately after His Baptism.

When He had been baptized, Jesus came up immediately from the water; and behold, the heavens were opened to Him, and He saw the Spirit of God descending like a dove and alighting upon Him. And suddenly a voice came from heaven, saying, "This is My beloved Son, in whom I am well pleased."

(Matthew 3:16-17)

The Father spoke again to the disciples of Jesus on the Mount of Transfiguration. The voice spoke out from the cloud saying, "This is my Beloved Son in whom I am well pleased; hear Him" (Matthew 17:5b). The last episode of

God's vocal testimony of His Son Jesus was shortly after He raised Lazarus from the dead. Jesus was troubled in spirit as He saw His death approaching.

> *"Father, glorify Your name." Then a voice came from heaven, saying, "I have both glorified it and will glorify it again." Therefore the people who stood by and heard it said that it had thundered. Others said, "An angel has spoken to Him." Jesus answered and said, "This voice did not come because of Me, but for your sake."*
>
> (John 12:28-30)

All the above testimonies and proclamations of Jesus by the Authority in heaven, people on earth, and spirits under the earth point to one thing. Jesus was not just an ordinary man, and His name was not and is not an ordinary name. The Apostle Paul, under the inspiration of the Holy Spirit, proclaimed the name of Jesus as the name above every other name, and at which every knee should bow and every tongue should confess that Jesus Christ is Lord to the glory of the Father.

Brethren, when you look at this cloud of witnesses, what does the name Jesus mean to you? What is the Spirit of God saying to you now about Jesus? God has given to us this name as a legacy that we should use it in our daily struggles against the forces of evil, against principalities and powers, and against spiritual wickedness in high and low places (Ephesians 6:12). You now have within you and in your mouth the power of His name to use to defeat the devil in every area of your life. Jesus is the word of power which we preach. All the words that Jesus spoke were words of power from heaven. Jesus' words were and still are very powerful. If you have not been getting results speaking your own words, you can now begin to speak the words of Jesus through your own mouth to your situation, and enjoy a better result. There is power in the name of Jesus. It is high time we began speaking the name of Jesus over our situations and believing in it as did the disciples, prophets, demons, angels, and God the Father Himself.

Chapter 5

Abiding in Christ

The secret of power is unconditional surrender to God, complete commitment to follow Jesus, and absolute trust in His name. According to Jesus it means abiding in the vine, "Abide in Me, and I in you. As the branch cannot bear fruit of itself, unless it abides in the vine, neither can you, unless you abide in Me. I am the vine, you are the branches. He who abides in Me, and I in him, bears much fruit; for without Me you can do nothing" (John 15:4).What does it mean to abide in Christ? To abide means to dwell, stay on, stay with, adhere to, agree to, obey, conform to, remain, continue, accept, tarry, reside, submit to, observe, follow, and put up with. These words and phrases describe the single word that Jesus chose to define, explain, and express the relationship between Him and His followers. I applaud His choice of words. The word abide is a powerful word. It evokes a sense of steadfastness, agreement, obedience, continuity, acceptance, staying together, and dwelling together. .

To get the best of what Jesus has to offer, you have to come **to Him** and remain **in Him**. Notice that He says **abide in Me** and **I in you**. That is more than a casual relationship. Every relationship, no matter how intimate, sweet, and strong, ends at some point. But the relationship that

Jesus is advocating here has no end, even in death it continues. Jesus does not only want us to abide in Him, He will equally abide in us. When He comes to abide in us, the Father also comes in with Him. The Father already abides in Jesus and they are inseparable. In essence you will have a double reinforcement of power, anointing, and grace when you invite Jesus to abide in you.

The secret of power is abiding in Him. Jesus says it is like the relationship between a vine (tree) and its branches. As long as the branch stays on the tree, it receives nourishment and support. But from the moment that the branch brakes off, it loses the vital nourishment necessary for its sustenance and existence. It can no longer fulfill its functions of bearing flowers and fruit and ultimately will die of starvation.

The same is true of every child of God and every disciple of Jesus Christ. The believer must of necessity abide strongly and continuously in Him to receive the needed spiritual life, support, and nourishment required for survival and fruitfulness. Jesus is that vine and we are the branches. Let us remain steadfastly plugged into Him. This life-giving support makes the believer much more fruitful. Jesus went on to say that without His abiding presence, the believer is powerless to do anything meaningful for the furtherance of the kingdom of God. We simply can do nothing, absolutely nothing on our own.

I believe Jesus is telling us that He does all the work in the life of a yielded child of God. In the Epistle to the Philippians Paul writes, "For it is God who works in you both to will and to do for His good pleasure" (Philippians 2:13). It is by His grace we are saved and sustained. "For by grace you have been saved through faith, and that not of yourselves; it is the gift of God, not of works, lest anyone should boast" (Ephesians 2:8-9).

Abiding steadfastly in Christ is the only way we can continuously access the life-giving grace we need to be fruitful for God. It is God who gives fruitfulness to our efforts and not by our strength alone. God works in us through Jesus to accomplish His purposes on earth as it is in heaven. We do not know how things are done in heaven, only He who is in heaven knows. He directs our steps according to our willingness to yield to His guidance. Therefore, abiding in Jesus is very crucial for the child of God.

Abiding in Christ has other ramifications for the believerIf you abide in Me, and My words abide in you, you will ask what you desire, and it shall be done for you" (John 15:7). Jesus here ties receiving answers to our prayer to our abiding in Him. In order words, our prayers receive His endorsement, favor, blessings, and answers when we are abiding in Him. If we are not abiding in Jesus, our prayers, petitions, and requests could be rejected or even be offensive to Him. He would not endorse them for immediate answers because He does not recognize them as coming from His own. This is a dangerous position to be with God. The secret of power is being joined together with Christ and remaining in Him; come what may.

Another benefit of abiding in Jesus is to enjoy His love and that of His Father. "As the Father loved Me, I also have loved you; abide in My love. If you keep My commandments, you will abide in My love, just as I have kept My Father's commandments and abide in His love" (John 15:9). You will not be able to go very far as a believer if you are not enjoying the love of Jesus. If you are in anyway living under the displeasure of Jesus, you are most certainly in trouble with the Father as well because they are one. You can not say you love God but do not like Jesus. Jesus said,

"I and My Father are one." Amend your walk with Jesus to receive all that God has in store for you. The secret of power is abiding in the love of Jesus.

Wonderful Blessings in the Name of Jesus

In the letter to the Ephesians, Paul wrote concerning the wonderful blessings we have inherited as a result of our believing Jesus Christ.

> *[For I always pray to] the God of our Lord Jesus Christ, the Father of glory, that He may grant you a spirit of wisdom and revelation [of insight into mysteries and secrets] in the [deep and intimate] knowledge of Him, By having the eyes of your heart flooded with light, so that you can know and understand the hope to which He has called you, and how rich is His glorious inheritance in the saints (His set-apart ones), and [so that you can know and understand] what is the immeasurable and unlimited and surpassing greatness of His power in and for us who believe, as demonstrated in the working of His mighty strength, Which He exerted in Christ when He raised Him from the dead and seated Him at His [own] right hand in the heavenly [places], far above all rule and authority and power and dominion and every name that is named [above every title that can be conferred], not only in this age and in this world, but also in the age and the world which are to come. And He has put all things under His feet and has appointed Him the universal and supreme Head of the church [a headship exercised throughout the church].*
> (Ephesians 1:17-22 AMP)

The Message Bible summarizes the blessings of this passage this way:

I ask—ask the God of our Master, Jesus Christ, the God of glory—to make you intelligent and discerning in knowing him personally, your eyes focused and clear, so that you can see exactly what it is he is calling you to do, grasp the immensity of this glorious way of life he has for his followers, oh, the utter extravagance of his work in us who trust him—endless energy, boundless strength! All this energy issues from Christ: God raised him from death and set him on a throne in deep heaven, in charge of running the universe, everything from galaxies to governments, no name and no power exempt from his rule. And not just for the time being, but forever. He is in charge of it all, has the final word on everything. At the center of all this, Christ rules the church. The church, you see, is not peripheral to the world; the world is peripheral to the church. The church is Christ's body, in which he speaks and acts, by which he fills everything with his presence."

(Ephesians 1:17-22)

There are so many wonderful blessings in Jesus Christ. Most of them are spiritual, some of them we can see and feel, others we cannot. The greatest of all blessings that humans can receive is the gift of salvation and the forgiveness of sin.

For whosoever shall call on the name shall be saved.

(Romans 10:13)

Neither is there salvation in any other: for there is none other name under heaven given among men, whereby we must be saved.

(Acts 4:12)

These are blessings that only God can give and are only possible through the name of Jesus. There is no other name like the name of Jesus. Peter also includes the blessings and power we have in Jesus Christ.

Simon Peter, a bondservant and apostle of Jesus Christ, To those who have obtained like precious faith with us by the righteousness of our God and Savior Jesus Christ: Grace and peace be multiplied to you in the knowledge of God and of Jesus our Lord, as His divine power has given to us all things that pertain to life and godliness, through the knowledge of Him who called us by glory and virtue, by which have been given to us exceedingly great and precious promises, that through these you may be partakers of the divine nature, having escaped the corruption that is in the world through lust.

(2 Peter 1:1-4)

The Message brings it out more clearly:

Simon Peter, a servant and apostle of Jesus Christ, To those who through the righteousness of our God and Savior Jesus Christ have received a faith as precious as ours: Grace and peace be yours in abundance through the knowledge of God and of Jesus our Lord. His divine power has given us everything we need for life and godliness through our knowledge of him who called us by his own glory and goodness. Through these he has given us his very great and precious promises, so that through them you may participate in the divine nature and escape the corruption in the world caused by evil desires.

(2 Peter 1:1-4)

There is safety in the name of the Lord. "The name of the Lord is a strong tower; the righteous run to it and are safe" (Proverbs 18:10). If you are oppressed by the enemy, the name of the Lord is a safe hiding place. When you need a shoulder to lean on, the name of the Lord is as soft as a pillow. It is a very present help in time of need. When you need a friend, Jesus is the best friend you can ever have. When there is a battle within or without, the name of the Lord will defend you. When you are unable to help yourself, the Lord will fight for you like He did for the children of Israel. At other times He is with you in battle, trouble or war. The Psalms are filled with many wonderful promises and blessings available to the child of God. Psalm 91:14-15 says, "Because he has set his love upon Me, therefore I will deliver him; I will set him on high, because he has known My name. He shall call upon Me, and I will answer him; I will be with him in trouble; I will deliver him and honor him." Psalm 20:1 says, "May the Lord answer you in the day of trouble; May the name of the God of Jacob defend you." The name of Jesus is a strong refuge in times of distress, trouble or disaster.

Power of the Holy Ghost

Power is released when you receive the Holy Ghost. "But you shall receive power when the Holy Spirit has come upon you" (Acts 1:8). You can only receive the Holy

Ghost or the gift of the Holy Ghost through the name of Jesus. Jesus gives the Holy Ghost only to those who believe. This special gift is not for everybody, it is only for those who have accepted Him as their personal Lord and Savor.

"But the Comforter, which is the Holy Ghost, whom the Father will send in my name, he shall teach you all things, and bring all things to your remembrance, whatsoever I have said unto you."

(John14:26)

And when he had said this, he breathed on them, and said unto them, "Receive ye the Holy Ghost."

(John 20:22)

The Holy Ghost activates the power of God within you. You need the Holy Spirit to activate the power of God in your life and ministry. If you are born again you can ask God for the gift of the Holy Ghost. Jesus is the only one that gives the gift of the Holy Ghost. Through the Holy Ghost the power of God is released and you can dramatically increase your spiritual potential.

Grace

Grace is the undeserved, unmerited, unconditional love and kindness that God has bestowed on the undeserving human race. Grace is God's greatest eternal blessing of richness and goodness dispensed by Jesus Christ. "For by grace you have been saved through faith, and that not of yourselves; it is the gift of God, not of works, lest anyone should boast" (Ephesians 2:8-9).Until Jesus came into the world, grace was a rare gift and sparsely distributed. The grace that we enjoy and take for granted in this dispensation was very rare in past dispensations. It used to be by special favor or anointing that people in the past received grace. Now the Word of God says, "For the law was given through Moses, but **grace and truth came through Jesus Christ**" (John 1:17). In Titus 2:11 it says, "For the grace of God that brings salvation has appeared to all men." Finally, "The grace of our Lord Jesus Christ be with you" (1 Thessalonians 5:28). May God bless you with the anointing of grace and favor. Jesus is an all-sufficient name. His grace is all-sufficient. It is good for all situations. It is ever present and ever ready. It is full of blessings, hope and faith that can make you stand strong. Paul wrote that God said to him, "My grace is sufficient for you, for My strength is made perfect in weakness" (2 Corinthians12:9). Paul was willing to face any of life's challenges because of the all sufficient grace God provided for him in every situation. When the name of Jesus goes before you it gives grace and favor. When Jesus follows behind you His grace brings goodness and mercy. When it resides in you it gives the light of salvation, eternal life, and truth. You cannot lose or go wrong relying on the name of Jesus in spirit and in truth. It is a trustworthy name. Trust it and it will give you favor all the days of your life. It is too big, too holy, and too powerful to fail.Jesus came to bring the grace that supersedes the law. There is liberty and empowerment in the grace of God. This is the grace that abolished the law and gave us direct unfettered access into the presence of the Most High. The power of sin is abolished in the dispensation of grace. (Read my book: "Grace Driven Life").

Chapter 6

Healing and Miracles in the Name of Jesus

The name of Jesus has absolute power to heal. Not just in Bible days, but also in the contemporary world and in the daily lives of Christians around the world that trust Him. In all major crusades and evangelistic meetings, healings and miracles do manifest themselves through the preaching of the name of Jesus. I have personally witnessed countless healings and miracles through the name of Jesus. I know without any shadow of doubt that there is healing power in the name of Jesus. You too can experience it if you trust Him and His word. "And His name, through faith in His name, has made this man strong, whom you see and know. Yes, the faith which comes through Him has given him this perfect soundness in the presence of you all" (Acts 3:16). Healing is readily available to everyone who believes in the name of the only begotten Son of God. Healing in the name of Jesus is not limited to physical healing. It includes emotional, spiritual, financial, and national healing too. The name of Jesus heals all types of sicknesses and diseases. It destroys ancestral curses, voodoo, and witchcraft manipulations. It heals infertility in those who have the faith to believe for their healing. Hebrews 11:6 warns us though that without faith it is impossible to please God or receive from God. In my ten years of ministering in Africa, we witnessed many healing miracles, and some bizarre demonic deliverances through the name of Jesus. For example, a friend of my wife reported that she had been told by her own doctor and three other prominent doctors that she could not have another child because she had an ovarian cyst. I had never heard of anything like that before that day. Needless to say I was disturbed and a bit confused, but we had faith and prayed together in the name of Jesus. She was wearing a big flowing gown so it was not possible to see how swollen her abdomen was, but when she gave me her permission to lay hands on her stomach to pray, I found it was bloated and hard. Nine months after that prayer of faith, the God who never fails manifested His power, and she delivered a healthy baby boy to the glory of the name of Jesus. Another woman wanted a child after more than three years of marriage. She and her husband joined our church and she was prayed for in one of our services to receive the fruit of the womb. Shortly after that she became pregnant but was constantly sick. She went to the hospital and was told by her doctor that the child was growing outside of the womb instead of inside the womb calling it an "ectopic pregnancy." She came straight from the hospital to our home. She was so devastated, broke down and wept bitterly. She was told that it would take a major surgery to deliver the child who had little chance of survival

My first reaction was to pray that God would reposition the child inside the womb, but she vehemently refused that saying she did not want the pregnancy anymore. When I asked what she wanted God to do for her, she repeated that she did not want to continue with this pregnancy. So we prayed and called on the name of Jesus asking God to take away the pregnancy. After the prayer she had peace and was strengthened. The next day she came running to our home to tell us that while she was having her bath, she felt something flowing down her legs. When she looked she saw lumps of blood and then everything flowed out. She was very happy and we praised and thanked God together. The next Sunday we prayed for her again in the name of Jesus and within weeks God gave her another pregnancy. She went on to have her baby to the glory of the blessed name of Jesus.

There was one miracle that surprised us but surely demonstrated the power of the name of Jesus. A family friend brought her out-of-state friend to our home one day with an unusual prayer request. The woman's friend was grossly obese, but she desperately wanted to lose weight and then marry. Though we thought it a strange request, she was very serious and wanted us to pray for her. . To me it was like Elisha asking for the double portion of Elijah's spirit.

As a preacher of faith that understood the power in the name of Jesus, I could not say no to a person who has faith for a healing miracle of any kind. I told her to sow a seed for her miracle, she sowed her widow's might, not a whole lot, but she was obedient.Then we prayed a prayer of agreement and they left.

About four months later, this same woman came to see me with someone I could not readily recognize and they were smiling as they approached me. I greeted them normally and they began to laugh. "Pastor the woman said, don't you remember this woman?" I shook my head and said "no I don't remember." They laughed the more.

Then she asked again, "don't you remember the woman you prayed for who wanted to loose weight and marry. I tried hard to remember but while I was struggling with my thoughts, the woman herself said "Pastor remember that you asked me to sow a seed for my miracle." I screamed and we hugged, praised God, and rejoiced together. Only God could have performed the miracle I was looking at in the life of that woman. The prayer of faith in the name of Jesus Christ produced a weight loss miracle in her life. This woman had lost so much weight I could not recognize her at the first. Moreover, She handed me an invitation to attend her wedding the following month. Till date that miracle still baffles me. It was a sure indication that there is nothing to hard for God to through Jesus Christ.

The name of Jesus is a life Changer.................

Another miracle we witnessed was with a pregnant member in our church whose fetus was breached. The baby was lying across instead of the normal position. In the final weeks of the pregnancy, she told my wife the problem she was facing and according to her it could take a Caesarian operation to deliver her baby safely. But she was afraid she could die in the process. She was the lone bread winner of the home, with two other children and an alcoholic husband. My wife encouraged her to come for deliverance prayers.

From the day we knew about her predicament, we continued praying for her until the day of delivery. Because of her situation, I asked my wife to accompany her to the hospital, and assured the woman to hold on to the name of Jesus and that she would deliver safely. As they were in the car on their way to the hospital, she noticed the baby moving in her womb. By the time they got to the hospital, her contractions were so intense that she was quickly rushed into the operating room, but before they could ready her for surgery she delivered a healthy baby boy.

These challenging stories testified to the power in Jesus name we witnessed during our ministry both in Africa and Canada that provided more evidence to us that there is miracle healing power in the name of Jesus. We saw about eleven women who had been declared infertile deliver children, at least two people were revived from death, others were delivered from wrongful incarcerations and arrests, and we witnessed a countless number of healings and powerful deliverances from demonic afflictions. We saw many, many souls give their lives to Jesus Christ, some are pastors today. There is undoubtedly, in the name of Jesus, a power that you need today and always for your healing. On a lighter note, one hilarious miracle that we witnessed was about a man who did not like his wife's flat buttocks. He told his wife to ask for prayer for a bigger one. She did, we prayed a prayer of agreement, and months later her buttocks began to grow. The last time I heard from her she was having problems trying to lose weight in that area. Jesus can turn any need or problem into a solution.

A male member of our church had not had a job for a long time because he had a drinking problem. He knew people in high places who could give him a job or help him get one, but because of his drinking problem they refused to help him. After he joined our church, God cleansed him and turned his life around for good. He decided he wanted to go into business for himself as a contractor. He brought his proposals and registration papers and we prayed over them in the name of Jesus before he submitted them. The very first contract he won was for over three hundred thousand Naira (Nigerian currency). That was a ton of money at the time. Jesus completely turned his life around.

This next miracle happened to our family. In the early days of the ministry things were a bit tough. We did not have enough money to buy meat for food so we were buying and eating mostly imported fish that was frozen and packaged called "ice fish." We did not have much choice though we did not particularly like ice fish. One day when I smelled the fish, I nearly threw up. I screamed at the top on my voice in desperation and frustration, "Oh! God I am sick and tired of eating ice fish all the time."

To my great surprise, even my desperate "prayer" was registered in heaven. The next Sunday two live goats were brought to our church by two women whose husbands were released from a Malaysian prison after our prayers for them. The goats were their way of thanking God for rescuing their husbands. Two weeks later another person whose prayer God answered brought his goat to us also. From that day ice fish ceased to appear on our table. God improved our condition tremendously. God did for us what He did for the children of Israel when they asked for meat in the desert. To the Immortal, Invisible, Omnipotent, and only Wise God be all the glory and honor and praise forever and ever. And to Jesus be all adoration through all eternity. Amen.

I can go on and on and on about our experiences with the healing and miracle power of God through the name of Jesus. I could write a whole book on this subject, but for now let me just say these proved that Jesus is still in the business of performing miracles and healing sicknesses and diseases today. Your case could be the next great story!

Fullness of Joy

Jesus told His disciples in John 16:24, "Until now you have asked nothing in My name. Ask, and you will receive, that your joy may be full" Jesus is interested in our happiness and joy here on earth. Joy is different from happiness. Happiness is dependent on happenstances like your mood, the weather, the condition of you bank account, good or bad news, and what you have or have not.Joy on the other hand, the joy that Jesus gives, is not dependent on any physical or external factors. It comes from the Spirit of God and resides in your spirit. It is a gift of God. It is so deep-seated that nothing from the external can disturb it, not even death or threat of death. Jesus wants to give you His joy

Peace in the Name of Jesus

"These things I have spoken to you, that in Me you may have peace. In the world you will have tribulation; but be of good cheer, I have overcome the world" (John 16:33). In the mist of this troubled world you can have peace, absolute perfect peace; peace that transcends your external circumstances and situation. This is a peace that cannot be bought with money. Peace is a legacy, an unquantifiable inheritance that Christ bequeathed only to those who believe in His name. "Peace I leave with you, My peace I give to you; not as the world gives do I give to you. Let not your heart be troubled, neither let it be afraid" (John 14: 27). Have you received this peace or are you still searching for it? Jesus gives unconditional peace. Call Him today, call Him now if you are going through a tough time.

Eternal Life

In ministering to the disciples Jesus said, "And I give them eternal life, and they shall never perish; neither shall anyone snatch them out of My hand" (John 10:28).

> *For God so loved the world that He gave His only begotten Son, that whoever believes in Him should not perish but have everlasting life.*
>
> (John 3:16)

> *"As You have given Him authority over all flesh, that He should give eternal life to as many as You have given Him. And this is eternal life, that they may know You, the only true God, and Jesus Christ whom You have sent".*
>
> (John 17:2-3)

Beloved, even if you do not need Jesus for any other reason, you definitely need Him for your eternal life. Jesus asked this question, "For what will it profit a man if he gains the whole world, and loses his own soul? Or what will a man give in exchange for his soul?" (Mark 8:36-37). Please call Him today to book your place. His number is: J-E-S-U-S. Do not wait until it is too late.

Chapter 7

Why Did Jesus Come?

We just learned that Jesus came to bring us the gift of eternal life. But there are many more reasons why Jesus came. We will explore some of those reasons in this chapter.

Give Power to the People

Before the advent of Jesus there was power in the world, but it was in the wrong hands. It was in the hands of Satan and his agents. Many of the kings in those ancient days had sorcerers, diviners, and satanic false prophets because they believed that the only way to get power was to worship Satan. That was the reason there was so much evil, darkness, oppression, and injustice in the world before the coming of Jesus. Idol worship was so prevalent that there had hardly been any major prophets or prophecies in the land of Israel for over 400 years before Jesus came. The world was so full of evil that God spoke through the prophets that Jesus would come to give light to the people who were living in such deep darkness.

For behold, the darkness shall cover the earth, and deep darkness the people; but the Lord will arise over you, and His glory will be seen upon you.

(Isaiah 60:2)

In the New Testament it was written that the Christ would bring light to them that were under the shadow of death.

Now when Jesus heard that John had been put in prison, He departed to Galilee. And leaving Nazareth, He came and dwelt in Capernaum, which is by the sea, in the regions of Zebulun and Naphtali, that it might be fulfilled which was spoken by Isaiah the prophet, saying: "The land of Zebulun and the land of Naphtali, by the way of the sea, beyond the Jordan, Galilee of the Gentiles: the people who sat in darkness have seen a great light, and upon those who sat in the region and shadow of death, Light has dawned." From that time Jesus began to preach and to say, "Repent, for the kingdom of heaven is at hand."

(Luke 4:12-17)

Evil was so prevalent in those days that not even the House of God (the Temple) in Jerusalem was spared. God had to take Ezekiel into the temple in a series of visions to show him what the leaders of the people and the priests where doing at night right inside the house of God.

And it came to pass in the sixth year, in the sixth month, on the fifth day of the month, as I sat in my house with the elders of Judah sitting before me, that the hand of the Lord God fell upon me there. Then I looked, and there was a likeness, like the appearance of fire—from the appearance of His waist and downward, fire; and from His waist and upward, like the appearance of brightness, like the color of amber. He stretched out the form of a hand, and took me by a lock of my hair; and the Spirit lifted me up between earth and heaven, and brought me in visions of God to Jerusalem, to the door of the north gate of the inner court, where the seat of the image of jealousy was, which provokes to jealousy. And behold, the glory of the God of Israel was there, like the vision that I saw in the plain.

Then He said to me, "Son of man, lift your eyes now toward the north." So I lifted my eyes toward the north, and there, north of the altar gate, was this image of jealousy in the entrance.

Furthermore He said to me, "Son of man, do you see what they are doing, the great abominations that the house of Israel commits here, to make Me go far away from My sanctuary? Now turn again, you will see greater abominations." So He brought me to the door of the court; and when I looked, there was a hole in the wall. Then He said to me, "Son of man, dig into the wall"; and when I dug into the wall, there was a door.

And He said to me, "Go in, and see the wicked abominations which they are doing there." So I went in and saw, and there—every sort of creeping thing, abominable beasts, and all the idols of the house of Israel, portrayed all around on the walls. And there stood before them seventy men of the elders of the house of Israel, and in their midst stood Jaazaniah the son of Shaphan. Each man had a censer in his hand, and a thick cloud of incense went up. Then He said to me, "Son of man, have you seen what the elders of the house of Israel do in the dark, every man in the room of his idols? For they say, 'The Lord does not see us, the Lord has forsaken the land.'"

And He said to me, "Turn again, and you will see greater abominations that they are doing." So He brought me to the door of the north gate of the Lord's house; and to my dismay, women were sitting there weeping for Tammuz (god/ goddess of sex & fertility).

Then He said to me, "Have you seen this, O son of man? Turn again, you will see greater abominations than these." So He brought me into the inner court of the Lord's house; and there, at the door of the temple of the Lord, between the porch and the altar, were about twenty-five men with their backs toward the temple of the Lord and their faces toward the east, and they were worshiping the sun toward the east.

And He said to me, "Have you seen this, O son of man? Is it a trivial thing to the house of Judah to commit the abominations which they commit here? For they have filled the land with violence; then they have returned to provoke Me to anger. Indeed they put the branch to their nose. Therefore I also will act in fury. My eye will not spare nor will I have pity; and though they cry in My ears with a loud voice, I will not hear them."

(Ezekiel 8:1-18)

Throughout these visions God showed Ezekiel the extent of the abominations and idolatry that were practiced even in the temple by the elders and leaders of the people of God—Israel. It was because of such practices that God repeatedly delivered them into captivity. The vision itself was in retrospect because Israel was already in captivity when God showed Ezekiel the vision. The world was ruled by Satan through witchcraft, sorcery, divination, and secret cults. Idol and satanic worship were the order of the day. Human and animal sacrifices with all kinds of abominable practices dominated such worship. Satan commanded the leaders and worshippers to drink blood and eat human flesh and if anyone refused, his blood would be the next.

Therefore God said to them, "Thus says the Lord God: You eat meat with blood, you lift up your eyes toward your idols, and shed blood. Should you then possess the land? You rely on your sword, you commit abominations, and you defile one another's wives. Should you then possess the land?"
(Ezekiel 33:25-26)

If a king needed power, he would go to the devil through one of his emissaries and mortgaged his own soul, the members of his family, and even his community depending on the amount of power he asked for. Survival of the fittest, dictatorship, authoritarianism, and brute force were weapons used to force people into submission. Injustice, inequality, slavery, prostitution, and wickedness ruled in the kingdoms and palaces. The whole world was held in retarding bondage and fear until Jesus came and destroyed the power of the devil. He broke the backbone and the authority of Satan and liberated man from the clutches of

Satan. Because of evil, blindness, and darkness, there was very little progress in human history from the time of Adam to Jesus. Man could not save or deliver himself. What could not be achieved for over 4,000 years of human existence would now be accomplished within a hundred years of the explosion of the gospel of Jesus Christ. What a testimony to the power and superior authority in the superior name of Jesus and the gospel of Christ.It was because of the idolatry, phallicism, and other abominable practices by men and women of Israel that of the forty kings of Israel, only a few of them actually lived, worshipped, and remained faithful to Jehovah, the one and only true and living God of Israel. Most of them worshipped Baal and the gods of the Canaanites, Amorites, etc. Now men and women everywhere who trust in the name of Jesus conduct exploits against the kingdom of Satan with impunity. At the mention of the name of Jesus even by the weakest of believers, Satan and his demons scramble away. You too have this power in you if you believe.

Destroy the Works of the Devil

Jesus came to destroy the works of the devil and give new life, power, and grace to the people of God. John the Apostle wrote, "He who sins is of the devil, for the devil has sinned from the beginning. For this purpose the Son of God was manifested, that He might destroy the works of the devil" (1 John 3:8). Not only did Jesus destroy the power and works of Satan, He also gave the same power to continue the destruction of Satan's kingdom to all those who would believe in His name.

Jesus Himself said, "The thief does not come except to steal, and to kill, and to destroy. I have come that they may have life, and that they may have it more abundantly" (John 10:10). This life includes freedom from fear and oppression, as well as the blessings of peace, joy, and prosperity through the power of the Holy Ghost. Anywhere the gospel of Jesus takes root there is always a noticeable progress in the quality of life, education, civilization, human rights, civil rights, and scientific advancement of His people. Wherever Jesus rules there is progress and peace, but wherever Satan rules there is always fear, backwardness, and anarchy. Jesus came to destroy the works of the devil.

Warn About Hell

Jesus came to warn us of hell and the dangers of spending eternity in hell. Jesus warns us that hell is a terrible place, so terrible that losing a hand, foot or any other part of our body cannot compare to living in hell for the rest of eternity.

If your hand causes you to sin, cut it off. It is better for you to enter into life maimed, rather than having two hands, to go to hell, into the fire that shall never be quenched— where their worm does not die and the fire is not quenched. And if your foot causes you to sin, cut it off. It is better for you to enter life lame, rather than having two feet, to be cast into hell, into the fire that shall never be quenched— where their worm does not die, and the fire is not quenched. And if your eye causes you to sin, pluck it out. It is better for you to enter the kingdom of God with one eye, rather than having two eyes, to be cast into hell fire— where their worm does not die and the fire is not quenched. (Mark 9: 43-48)

Save Us from Sin

Jesus came to save us from sin, sickness, and evil. Sin is a killer. Sin is a destroyer both here and in eternity. The good news is that Jesus saves us from any sin or guilt. You do not have to carry your sin any longer. Jesus is our sin bearer. Sin is a heavy load. Give it up to Him now and you will receive peace and freedom instead. Call Him Now-JESUS.

> *For the Son of man is not come to destroy men's lives but to save them.*
>
> (Luke 9: 56)

> *This is a faithful saying and worthy of all acceptance, that Christ Jesus came into the world to save sinners, of whom I am chief.*
>
> (1 Timothy 1:15)

> *And we have seen and testify that the Father has sent the Son as Savior of the world.*
>
> (1 John 4:14)

Tell the Truth and Expose Satan

Jesus came to tell us the truth about God and to expose the fallacies of Satan. Jesus said, "In My Father's house are many mansions; if it were not so, I would have told you. I go to prepare a place for you. And if I go and prepare a place for you, I will come again and receive you to Myself; that where I am, there you may be also" (John 14: 2-3). Concerning Satan Jesus said to the Jews, "You are of your father the devil, and the desires of your father you want to do. He was a murderer from the beginning, and does not stand in the truth, because there is no truth in him. When he speaks a lie, he speaks from his own resources, for he is a liar and the father of it" (John 8:44). God is good. Jesus is His active operational name. Call Him today for help.

Chapter 8

Jesus, God In the Flesh

In the Gospel of John it says,"And the Word became flesh and dwelt among us, and we beheld His glory, the glory as of the only begotten of the Father, full of grace and truth" (John 1:14).And in 1 Timothy 3:16 Paul writes, "And without controversy great is the mystery of godliness: God was manifested in the flesh, Justified in the Spirit, seen by angels, Preached among the Gentiles, Believed on in the world, Received up in glory." Jesus is Emmanuel: God with us.As God in the flesh, Jesus came to reveal the Godhead, make Himself known to men, and to live among men forever. Jesus lives in the hearts of believers by faith so that there will no longer be any broken communication with Him. There will no longer be the need for man to say, "Where is my God?" Jesus came so that man may be as close to Him as possible.

Help Man's Weaknesses

Jesus came to help man in his weaknesses and struggles against sin and evil. Jesus said, "Come to Me, all you who labor and are heavy laden, and I will give you rest" (Matthew 11:28). God told Paul, "My grace is sufficient for you, for My strength is made perfect in weakness" (2 Corinthians 12:9). You are a child of God therefore you are not alone in your struggles. Jesus is there with you and within you to assist you when you call Him.

Open Blind Eyes

Jesus came to open blind eyes and heal spiritual ignorance. All the years that man was under the dictatorship of the devil, man was blinded to the truth of the Word of God and the power within him. He was in both spiritual blindness and spiritual ignorance. Paul writes, "This I say, therefore, and testify in the Lord, that you should no longer walk as the rest of the Gentiles walk, in the futility of their mind, having their understanding darkened, being alienated from the life of God, because of the ignorance that is in them, because of the blindness of their heart" (Ephesians 4:17-18). Spiritual ignorance is the worst kind of ignorance because it robs you of your greatest source of power and a good relationship with your Creator. Spiritual ignorance makes people live in fear of things that should serve and fear them. Spiritual ignorance has made people live today like there is no tomorrow or eternity. Are you still ignorant of the grace of God? Jesus is the light of the world. Allow Him to shine God's light on your darkness and come and show you the way into the light.

Reveal God's Love

Jesus came to reveal God's love. "For God so love the world that He gave His only begotten Son, that whosoever believes in Him should not perish but have everlasting life" (John 3:16). Jesus also said, "Greater love has no one than this, than to lay down one's life for his friends" (John

15:13). Jesus is God's love personified. He embodied all that God was and is and is to come. Jesus demonstrated the love of God as no other man could. You need the love of God in your life today. Call J-E-S-U-S now.

Die as a Ransom

Jesus came to die as a ransom. According to Him, "For even the Son of Man did not come to be served, but to serve, and to give His life a ransom for many" (Mark 10:45). God believed that the only way to secure the freedom of mankind from the dominion of Satan was to redeem him by dying to atone for the sins of the world. This is a mystery. We cannot fully understand why God chose to do that until we meet Him in eternity. Through Jesus, God has released man to have the freedom, power, and grace to be and achieve all that his heart desires for his ultimate good.

Salvation is free for all. You can be saved even now if you will ask Jesus to forgive your sins, come into your heart, and be your Lord and Savior.

Reveal the Kingdom of God

Jesus came to teach us about the kingdom of God and the kingdom principles of love, faith, righteousness, forgiveness, and giving. Before Jesus came, a great majority of the people knew more about the kingdom, power, and worship of Satan than they did about God. Almost all the world worshipped Satan. They called him the god of this world even in the days of Jesus. Satan even demanded Jesus to worship him as king of the world.

Again, the devil took Him up on an exceedingly high mountain, and showed Him all the kingdoms of the world and their glory. And he said to Him, "All these things I will give You if You will fall down and worship me." Then Jesus said to him, "Away with you, Satan! For it is written, 'You shall worship the Lord your God, and Him only you shall serve'."

(Matthew 4:8-10)

Jesus started His ministry by preaching repentance as a way to learn, know, possess, and inherit the kingdom of God."Repent, for the kingdom of heaven is at hand" (Matthew 4:17).This same message holds the key to the knowledge of the kingdom of heaven. He came to equip us for eternity with God in His kingdom.

Show Forgiveness

Jesus came to show us that God forgives sin and to teach us to forgive. He spent much of His earthly ministry teaching about and actually forgiving men and women of their sins.

But that you may know that the Son of Man has power on earth to forgive sins—then He said to the paralytic, "Arise, take up your bed, and go to your house." And he arose and departed to his house.

(Matthew 9:6-7)

And forgive us our debts, as we forgive our debtors. For if you forgive men their trespasses, your heavenly Father will also forgive you. But if you do not forgive men their trespasses, neither will your Father forgive your trespasses.

(Matthew 6:11-12, 14-15)

Practicing forgiveness is very crucial in maintaining an active relationship with God. It is a cardinal factor in all spiritual healing. Without forgiveness you will deny yourself peace, fullness of joy, and the love of God. The devil exploits this evil to torment people.

> *Then Peter came to Him and said, "Lord, how often shall my brother sin against me, and I forgive him? Up to seven times?" Jesus said to him, "I do not say to you, up to seven times, but up to seventy times seven."*
>
> (Matthew 18:21-22)

Jesus forgave the woman caught in adultery. He forgave Peter after he denied Jesus during His trial by the Jewish authorities. He forgave Paul on his way to Damascus to arrest and kill believers. He forgave the Jews and the Roman soldiers that crucified Him saying, "Father forgive them for they know not what they do." He forgave the thief on the cross even as He hung on the cross Himself. The list goes and on and on. The gospels are replete with the message and acts of forgiveness by Jesus. Forgiveness, in all its ramifications, was one of the cardinal reasons for Jesus coming to earth. A song writer sang it this way: "Have you been to Jesus for the cleansing power? Are you washed in the blood of the Lamb? Are you fully trusting in His grace this hour? Are you washed in the blood of the Lamb?"

Do the Will of God

Jesus came to do the will of God. He came to obey the Word of God and fulfill all the prophecies concerning Him. There were many prophesies in the Old Testament concerning the Messiah, the Anointed One. Those prophecies must be fulfilled for the Word of God to remain authentic, and for God not to become a liar in the eyes of the world. It was only a question of time before Jesus was revealed to fulfill these prophecies because the Word of God cannot fail. He came to show us that full obedience to the Word of God was and is possible today.

Restore Man's Relationship with God

Jesus came to show mankind the way back to God. He came to seek and to save that which was lost (Luke 19:10). Jesus said, "I am the Way, the Truth and the Life: no man comes to the Father, but by me" (John 14:6). In Isaiah 53:6 it says, "All we like sheep have gone astray; we have turned, every one, to his own way; and the Lord has laid on Him the iniquity of us all." God wants His erring and wayward children to come back to Him, therefore He sent Jesus to show us the way.

Proclaim the Good News

Jesus came to shine the light of the glorious good news. He said, "I have come as a light into the world, that who-ever believes in Me should not abide in darkness" (John 12:46).The light that Jesus brings is the light that leads to the forgiveness of sin and to eternal life. It is the light of love and grace. Jesus is the light of the world, the light of civilization, and the light of our conscience. The absence of the true light of God through Jesus Christ leads to our spiritual death. John wrote, "But if we walk in the light as He is in the light, we have fellowship with one another, and the blood of Jesus Christ His Son cleanses us from all sin" (1 John 1:7). Jesus gives true light to all those who come to Him.

Victorious Life

Among other great missions, Jesus came to give us the power and ability to live a victorious life in this world and to rise again when we fall. Many of us Christians live in defeat in many areas of our lives. This is due in part to ignorance of the awesome power within us, the power that is in the name of Jesus Christ. Jesus said, "Behold, I give you the power (authority) to trample on serpents and scorpions, and over all the power of the enemy, and nothing shall by any means hurt you" (Luke 10:19).This declaration is a very powerful statement. The power is already given, it is right now available, so why are we not using it? John the Apostle gives us the answer. "For whatever is born of God overcomes the world. And this is the victory that has overcome the world—our faith" (1 John 5:4). If you are born again, you have the seed of that power within you. Whether it's the power to succeed, get healed, defeat the devil or do any other exploit, the power is right inside of you.

Chapter 9

How to Use the Name of Jesus

B efore we go to the how-to part of this chapter, there is one more mystery I would like to help you unravel. Many have asked, "Where is the secret place of the Most High?"

The Secret Place of the Most High

Most Christians have read Psalm 91:1-2, "He who dwells in the secret place of the Most High shall abide under the shadow of the Almighty. I will say of the Lord, He is my refuge and my fortress; My God, in Him I will trust'." But the question is where is this secret place of the Most High? Another scripture that is of great importance to the child of God is found in Proverbs 18: 10,"The name of the Lord is a strong tower; the righteous run to it and are safe." These two scriptures hold the key to our under-standing of where the secret place of the Lord is.In the chapter on abiding in Christ, we said that abiding includes among other things "dwelling." It is no surprise that Jesus chose the word abide, which also means to dwell. He that abides also dwells. When Jesus said abide in me and I in you, He was telling us that if we will dwell in Him, He will dwell in us. The person that dwells in the secret place of the Most High dwells in Jesus and Jesus in him. We have learned that the name of Jesus is strong and powerful and too big to fail. It is as strong and as solid as a fortress. From the forgoing I believe that it will not be too much of a stretch to connect the dots and know that the secret place of the Most High is in the Name of Jesus. Therefore, the next time you read Proverbs 18:10 try reading it this way, "The name of the Lord Jesus is a strong tower and the righteous run into it and are safe. And also try substituting "place" "with the name of Jesus" in Psalm 91:1. The name of Jesus is stronger and more solid than any earthly fortress. It is the cornerstone of the Lord's house—the church. The Bible explains that whoever falls on the Stone which is Jesus, shall be broken to pieces, but he whom the Stone shall fall upon, shall be crushed to powder (Matthew 21:44). The name of Jesus now stands in the place of the risen Lord. We can do exceedingly, abundantly, over and above what the Lord could do while in the flesh, according to the power He has put in us. This is because He was limited in some ways by time, space, and people's unbelief when He was here in the flesh. But now His name knows no bounds, has no limitations, and has no fears or foes.

How to Use the Name of Jesus

The permission to use the name of Jesus in the Christian circles is a given. But what seems to not be the norm is seeing results after the use of the most powerful name in heaven and earth. So why are we not seeing miracles as they did in the early church? Does God hear us when we pray or call on the name of Jesus? Can we be sure that we will receive whatever we request or must someone with a greater faith pray or help us in prayer? Why do some of us not get an answer when we pray?

These and other questions are being asked everyday even by good Christian people. I do not believe that there is one answer that fits everybody's need when it comes to answers to prayers. However, let us examine some of the factors that can militate against our prayers.

Results from using the name of Jesus depend on the motive, state of mind, and obedience to the Word of God. Use of the name of Jesus must include asking in faith, without the interference of fear, doubt, unbelief, or impatience. The actions and utterances after the use of His name can also determine our results.

Motive

God judges the heart and looks at our motives. God cares about our reason for wanting a particular thing. The Bible says in 1 Samuel 16:7, "For the Lord does not see as man sees; for man looks at the outward appearance, but the Lord looks at the heart." The motive of our actions and our prayers are weighed before God. They determine whether our prayers will be answered in full or in part.I believe that God answers every prayer, but not in the same way. God may answer "yes" to some prayers, "no" to others, "wait" or hold on because it's not the right time. Whatever the answer, the motive behind the prayer is an important determining factor in the results received. If you are continually receiving a "no or wait answer" to a certain prayer, you may want to check your motive for making the request. I am talking to myself here as well.

During the process of editing this book someone asked me this question, "How do you know that a prayer merits a favorable answer from God?" I believe every prayer prayed according to the will of God and for the glory of God merits a favorable response. For example, prayer for healing or prosperity is covered by the will of God. However, only God determines which prayer and what time He will answer a prayer if our motives are right. My message is for us to be sure of our motives and God will unfailingly do His part.

A wrong motive is a sure "no" to most prayers. God wants to bless people whose motives are right or righteous before Him, not before their own eyes or before the eyes of the world. God wants His will to be done in our lives. He wants to bless the man or woman whose heart is after God's heart like a man who will use God's blessing to help others and advance His Kingdom.

God does not always bless us only for ourselves but for the benefit of others. God wants to bless us so we can be a blessing to others around us. God gives us more so we can distribute and share with others. The motive of every prayer is crucial to the response we receive from God.

State of the Mind

To a large extent, the state of your mind and that of the person you are praying with will shape the destiny of that prayer. How prepared are you for the things you are asking for? How ready are you to receive what you are praying for? Emotions play a great role in shaping and packaging our prayers to God. Some of them include: love, enthusiasm, joy, peace, sincerity, fear, anger, hatred, hypocrisy, guilt, sadness, bitterness, unforgiveness, indecision, doubt, pride, jealousy, arrogance, indifference, negative attitude, failure mentality, faith, and definiteness of purpose.

Many prayers are answered at the time and point of prayer. Therefore, the emotions in play at the time of prayer will determine how that prayer is received and answered in heaven. We should always present our prayers, petitions, and requests with the best of intentions and purposes.

There are many biblical evidences of real time answers to prayers. Elijah prayed for God to honor him and his sacrifice in 1 Kings18:30-38. God answered him then and there. He also prayed that fire should come down from heaven and consume the fifty soldiers sent to arrest him. Fire consumed the soldiers; not once but twice at the same place and in real time (2 Kings 1:10-12). Gideon's prayer included a fleece which God answered not once but twice in the same place (Judges 6:36-39). In Acts 5:1-9, Peter prayed for the cripple at the Beautiful Gate in the name of Jesus and received an immediate answer.

We should have the same attitude we would if we were taking that same request to a head of state or the Queen of England. You would no doubt agree with me that everyone who goes to see the Queen puts his or her best self forward: happy, cheerful, decorum, good intentions, respectful, polite, and so on. God is greater than any queen or king; God is holier than any president. God can read your state of mind even though the queen can not. Our physical or outward appearances are important, but not nearly as vital as the condition of our hearts.

Faith, love, enthusiasm, definiteness of purpose, gratitude, and joy play significantly more positive roles in the speed and measure of the answers to our prayers than any of the other listed emotions. God wants us to come into His presence with thanksgiving, praise, joy, and rejoicing and into His court or throne room with boldness or faith.

Serve the Lord with gladness; Come before His presence with singing. Know that the Lord, He is God;

It is He who has made us, and not we ourselves; we are His people and the sheep of His pasture. Enter into His gates with thanksgiving, and into His courts with praise. Be thankful to Him, and bless His name. For the Lord is good; His mercy is everlasting, And His truth endures to all generations."

(Psalm 100:1-5)

Paul writes about the same thing, "But without faith it is impossible to please Him, for he who comes to God must believe that He is, and that He is a rewarder of those who diligently seek Him. Let us therefore come boldly to the throne of grace that we may obtain mercy and find grace to help in time of need" (Hebrews 11:6, 4:16). It is important that the emotions of our heart at the time of prayer are pleasing to God.**Faith** is the medium of exchange in heaven and in the spiritual realm the same way money is here on earth. Without money we can not buy or transact earthly business. Without faith we cannot transact any kind of heavenly business. We can neither give nor receive anything from God without faith. Without faith it is impossible to please Him. The extent of one's faith determines what one can purchase from God. Faith is the currency with which we trade with God. Little faith buys little and large faith buys a lot.

You are richer than you think if you are a man or woman of faith. Faith comes by hearing the Word of God (Roman 10:17). Faith is an emotion and a spiritual gift. You need them both in play when praying, though you don't necessarily need to be concerned about which one you are using at the time of prayer. They sort themselves out when you pray. God wants to see enthusiastic faith in you at all times, especially when you pray.

If you are a child of God you already have a measure of faith and it will grow as you continually exercise your faith. All you need to do is to show your faith to God by trusting and believing His Word unconditionally for that situation you are praying about. Show Him you love and trust Him through your faith in His Word.

Obedience to His Word

There is nothing that gladdens the heart of God as when He sees faith in His Word. When we believe the Word of God, we believe God. When we doubt the Word we doubt God. When we believe the word, we believe Jesus, and when we believe Jesus we believe God. The Father, Son (Jesus the Word) and the Spirit are inseparable; God is spirit and Jesus is the living Word.

Most of those who obey the Word of God have faith in the God of the Word. Although there are some who obey out of fear of God's judgment or punishment. God does not want us to come to Him out of fear. God wants us to be "faith-full" and not "fear-full." Fear-full people hardly ever have their prayers answered. They live by works trying to please God. God does not want our self-righteousness. He said our righteousness is like filthy rags before Him. "But we are all like an unclean thing, and all our righteousnesses are like filthy rags; we all fade as a leaf, and our iniquities, like the wind, have taken us away" (Isaiah 64:6). Such people work in the flesh not faith, "So then, those who are in the flesh cannot please God" (Romans 8:8). God has provided salvation by faith through the atoning and finished work of Christ. "For by grace you have been saved through faith, and that not of yourselves; it is the gift of God, not of works, lest anyone should boast" (Ephesians 2:8-9).Knowledge of and faith in the Word of God gets God's attention and gets our prayers answered. There is tremendous power beneath the surface of the Word. Therefore, obeying the Word is releasing that power to work for you.

Actions After Prayer

Our actions or inaction immediately after prayer can play a significant role in seeing the results we expect. This is very important especially when we pray a prayer of faith or a power prayer where we expect an immediate response for from heaven. A corresponding action follows almost every power prayer. Nothing may happen until a corresponding action for that prayer takes place. The corresponding action could come from either the person praying or the person receiving the prayer or from both parties. The result could be delayed indefinitely until either the prayer is cancelled by unbelief or it is acted upon to actualize it.

For example, in Acts 3:6-7 when Peter asked the lame man at the Beautiful Gate to rise up and walk, he then took the man's hand and helped him to his feet. The Apostle Paul had a similar encounter in Lystra.

And in Lystra a certain man without strength in his feet was sitting, a cripple from his mother's womb, who had never walked. This man heard Paul speaking. Paul, observing him intently and seeing that he had faith to be healed, said with a loud voice, "Stand up straight on your feet!" And he leaped and walked. Now when the people saw what Paul had done, they raised their voices, saying in the Lycaonian language, "The gods have come down to us in the likeness of men!"

(Acts 14:8-10)

In this case Paul perceived that the lame man had faith to be healed. When Paul told him to rise up and walk, the man acted on the word of Paul, and jumped to his feet. That was the action required to actualize his healing. The action always follows the last word or command of the servant of God. There are many such incidences in the Scriptures, especially in Jesus' ministry. Jesus and those He healed followed these patterns also.

Utterances After Prayer

Words are powerful, words are living things. They can create and they can destroy. It is commonly said that "confession brings possession." What we say or confess after we have prayed, determine whether the prayer is strengthened or cancelled. The first confession after a prayer is made is very important. Imagine that you have just finished praying with a man of God and he asks you how you feel. If you say, "I'm still very terrible," while the angel that came to take or bring the answer to the prayer of faith is still standing there. What have you done? You have just cancelled the faith of the man of God who prayed with you. This is because the prayer was not mixed with your faith as you received and heard the prayer.

> *For indeed the gospel was preached to us as well as to them; but the word which they heard did not profit them, not being mixed with faith in those who heard it."*

> (Hebrew 4:2)

If you looked at the face of the man of God after you said such a negative thing after prayer, you would not see joy or praise to seal the prayer. You would see only disgust.

But if you had said, "I'm healed in the name of Jesus," then you would have heard him exclaim, "Praise the Lord!" That declaration seals the prayer and God is glorified even before He does the work. That puts God in an awkward situation because He has taken the praise without doing any work. God becomes a debtor to you. Since God is no man's debtor, He will pay what He owes. He will heal you. You are better off if you have God owing you than you owing Him.On the other hand when the prayer is cancelled by your confession, the angel who came to carry the prayer to God is left with nothing. The faith that should have accompanied the prayer, both yours and the man of God, has been nullified by your utterance or confession. Therefore the prayer is not answered. This is a hypothetical situation but it can be real.

Use of the Name

In Exodus 20:7 it says, "You shall not take the name of the Lord your God in vain, for the Lord will not hold him guiltless who takes His name in vain." The name of Jesus is a holy and most excellent name. Improper use of the name could even become sin against you if you do not give God the glory due His name. Improper use of the name of Jesus is like what the seven sons of Sceva did in Acts 19:14-16. They wanted to cast out devils and were themselves confronted by the devil and attacked because they did not properly use the name of Jesus.The name of Jesus is given to help us in our daily struggles and in the battles of life. God said through David in Psalm 111:9, "Holy and reverend is His name." We must give Him all the greatness, glory, honor, praise, and worship, adoration, and recognition due His mighty name. Use the name properly and you will see His glory.

Chapter 10

Battling the Giants

Since we have learned that God has given us the power and authority to use the name of Jesus to do battle against any circumstance or situation in our lives, why aren't more Christians walking in that power on an every day basis? It is because we have not been able to defeat the giants that try to steal our victory.

We know of the story of the young shepherd boy who defeated the mighty giant, Goliath. How was such a boy able to come against such a mighty foe and gain the victory? He refused to allow anyone, even the king, to persuade him that this giant was more powerful than God. David's biggest battle was not really against the giant. If he had not been able to stand against doubt, unbelief, and fear in his own heart and in those around him, he would not have been victorious when it came time to face Goliath. The giants we must defeat are inside of us and in the people we allow to speak into our lives.

The Giant Named Doubt

The emotions of doubt and unbelief are perhaps the most subtle of all emotions. Unbelief arises as a result of doubt and doubt as a result of insecurity and lack of assurance or faith. Both come from ignorance or lack of adequate information and knowledge concerning the faithfulness of God. Both have a debilitating influence on our faith. Doubt says, "I am not sure God is there. I am not sure I can trust Him with my life. I am not sure He is capable of helping me. I am not sure He will accept me. I am not sure He can change what the doctors have told me. This sickness has no cure. I am not righteous enough. I have not prayed enough. I am a sinner and God wouldn't hear me. I have prayed before and nothing happened. I am not sure I have enough faith. I am not sure I can even try."

The predominant phrase here is "I am not sure." When you are insecure or undecided you doubt, and when you doubt God's ability and capability, your faith stumbles. With all these doubts racing through your mind at the time of prayer, it is difficult to concentrate and muster enough courage and assurance within you to believe that you will receive your petition. Do not doubt God, take Him at His Word. There's a question that arose in this area of doubt and unbelief. "In the event of terminal illness that will inevitably lead to death, is it possible to distinguish the outcome of terminal illness and the avoidance of death based on faith? Why do believers suffer cancer and death like unbelievers?"

I will answer these questions based on my own understanding of the Word of God and God's dealings with me in the area of sicknesses, diseases, and healing. In my life time God has healed me of a countless number of sicknesses. Now if any sickness comes on me, I will just say, this too will go away or pass away. As I was reasoning this question with the person that asked it, I reminded him of the time I called him asking about the implications of a very low

White Blood Cells (WBC) in my blood. He is a medical doctor and his response was that cancer was a possibility among other things.

When I heard that my first reaction was a paralyzing fear, which is what kills so many people that have been diagnosed with cancer or other terminal illnesses. I had already been scheduled for a biopsy before I received his diagnosis. It took me some time to process my fears and come to terms with my reality. But I remembered God's faithfulness to me and the numerous people God had healed through my ministry. I decided that I was not going to succumb to the devil or to any sickness. I refused to give power and momentum to my fears.

I have seen God heal death twice. So I prepared for war against cancer or any eventuality. I decided that I was not going to do the biopsy. On the appointment day I was ushered into the room by the doctor. I looked him straight in the eyes and told him that I would not do it. He asked me why. I told him that I have a greater healer. He thought I was just afraid so he left and sent a nurse in to calm me down and persuade me to do the biopsy. After a long discussion with the nurse, she left and told the doctor all that I had said. The doctor said I could go home, but whenever I was ready I was welcome to come back. I told him I would never come again, and in my heart I added, and I will not die of cancer either.

What I did was to stop him from declaring me a cancer patient. I declared to myself that I was healed in Jesus name. I repeated that over and over as I was driving home. I came home that day and my faith rose up. I believed God for healing, prayed day and night without any fear of cancer or death. I knew that God answers prayers. I knew that God heals all manner of sicknesses and diseases. I knew He had healed me before, and I believed He would heal me again. I held onto my faith and disarmed my fears.

Secondly, I had read something about healing any sickness with water so I began to soak my life with prayer and water everyday. Six months later I went for another test and there was no sign of low WBC. Three months later I went again for another test and my WBC was still good. That ended the story. I believe if I had chosen to give into fear, doubt, and unbelief, the story would've been different today. I praise God for His grace and mercy upon my life. That is why I believe that no sickness, cancer or death can defeat a child of God who knows how to use the name of Jesus and stand on the authority of the promises of God.

Doubt is a faith destroyer. If you can not trust God in your heart, you do not trust Him at all no matter what else you do outwardly or whatever bold face or appearances you put on. "God is spirit, those that worship Him must worship Him in spirit and in truth" (John 4:24). Faith is in the heart and not in one's appearance. Faith is also acting·on what we believe. Doubting at the time of prayer is questioning God's integrity. It is placing your belief in something else other than God. Doubting is so subtle that you hardly notice that it is there most of the time. Sometimes it disguises itself in what seems like a rational thinking, educated or informed reasoning, or an expert opinion. But none of these are based on the Word of God. The Word of God is our final authority in matters of faith. Faith is never taught in public schools and so cannot be generated from text books.

The Giant Named Unbelief

Doubt when it is perfected gives birth to unbelief. Unbelief is the highest form of doubt. It consciously doubts or questions the existence of God, the integrity of God, and the veracity of the Word of God. It doubts everything that faith stands for and so closes the mind to the supernatural power of faith in the name Jesus and the Word of God. Unbelief says, "It's not possible. I don't or can't believe it." The children of Israel in their unbelief asked Moses in the wilderness. "Can God furnish a table in the wilderness? Can He provide meat for the people?" (Psalm 78:19-20).God is spirit and prayer is a spiritual communication exercise with God. You can not reason it all out with your finite human mind. Prayer is in the realm of the spirit and no human mind can fathom the mystery of it. It is done in faith and by faith. It is completely and absolutely faith based. It is either by faith or not at all. The reason we fail in prayer many a time is because we try to reason out spiritual things with our human intelligence and that creates doubt because faith transends human reasoning. This problem is more common with men than with women. People who have some form of higher education seek to intellectualize things, while the so called ignorant may find it easier to believe the things of the spirit. I am not knocking good education. I'm saying that rational reasoning makes us want to reason God out. God is too big for our small minds to reason out. We should accept what He says of Himself. There is no other way of proving prayer or other spiritual things than by acting on the Word of God. People who cannot reason out God in their finite minds conclude it does not work or there is no God or that He does not answer prayers. When they reach that conclusion they allow doubt and unbelief to keep them from God and spiritual blessings. Let me say here unequivocally that the spiritual world is as real as the physical. We do not understand how the moon and all the constellations of nature came to be suspended in the space indefinitely. He who claims to have put them there says, "Call upon me and I will answer you and show you great and mighty things which you do not know" (Jeremiah 33:3). Where there is deep seated doubt and unbelief, there is fear, apprehension or distrust. In other words, unbelief produces fear and fear is a destroyer. It destroys faith. I need to clarify here that there is a difference between faith and hope. Hope is futuristic while faith is now. Hope will see an answer in some unspecified future time, but faith brings immediate results. There is a place for hope. Hope shapes our future. Hope works our destiny, but faith answers our prayer now. For the purposes of our discussion we want our prayers to be answered now. Unbelief and doubt are major hindrances to our "now" prayers. You should not waste your time praying for what you don't believe. For that matter, there is no use praying in the name of Jesus if you don't believe in Him. My prayer for you today is that you will receive the grace of faith instead of unbelief.

The Giant Named Fear

Fear is a spiritual state of the mind. Fear is also a complex emotion that controls the mind, the brain, and in some ways the central nervous system. It can cripple your faith, your body systems, and your organs. It can reduce your reasoning capacity and confuse your brain. Fear can also create images, imaginations, contortions, and distortions in your spiritual, emotional and physical functions. It can cause your body to act or react in a manner that could be detrimental to your health and overall well being. The good news is fear can be controlled.Fear is a product of extreme doubt, unbelief, and hopelessness. There is always hope in God. Fear releases doubt in God and consequently in your own ability to handle the circumstance or situation confronting you. It portends helplessness that there is nothing or nobody else, at the spur of the moment, to help. A good question came up as we reviewed this book. "Does fear really exist?" It underscores the fact that some people do not believe that there is a spirit called fear just as others do not want to believe in miracles. To answer the question, we need to turn to the Word of God. I noticed that every sudden encounter between God or the angels and man was preceded by the phrase, "Fear not." When God was about to bless Abram in Genesis 15:1 He said to him first, "Fear not..." When God spoke to Joseph concerning Mary's pregnancy, the angel said to him, "Fear not" (Matthew 1:20). In 2 Timothy 1:7 the Bible says, "For God has not given us the spirit of fear but of power, of love and of a sound mind."

Fear is from the pit of hell. It is Satan's key weapon to control the mind of people. Wherever or whenever you sense or experience fear, there is something or someone that wants to control our mind. Fear exists but should we fear it? The Bible enjoins us to overcome fear with faith. For a complete list of the "Fear nots" in the Bible and how to deal with and overcome fear, read my book, "The Amazing Power of Grace ."

Fear raises unbelief in God, in His ability, willingness, speed, power, knowledge, and wisdom enough to change our circumstance or situation. It causes negativity around us and negative attitudes toward self and others. Fear says, "I'm afraid. I can't. God can't either." Whenever you say you can't, you will never be able to do that thing until you change your confession. The prayer of faith is the best antidote to fear that I know of. There is no fear in faith. It's either fear or faith, it can't be both. We over come fear by the action of faith. Pray when you are afraid. Sometimes it is possible to start out in fear and end with faith; not the other way round.

Impatience and Anxiety

Impatience and anxiety can rob us of the blessing of answered prayer. God is Sovereign. No one can dictate to Him how, where, and when He should answer our prayer. Our impatience or anxiety does not move God. However, it has been proven time and time again in the Scriptures that faith can and did move Him to compassion and action. Job 14:14 says, "I will wait till my change comes." We need to learn to wait on God with praise and thanksgiving for the situation we are praying or believing God for. One thing is sure, God is never late. If He didn't show up when you needed Him, He probably did something for you which you couldn't see at that time because you were preoccupied with your own small piece of the world. Anxiety can make us say or do things that are dishonoring to the name of God. There is virtue in waiting on God. In Isaiah 40:31 it says, "But those who wait on the Lord shall renew their strength; they shall mount up with wings as eagles, they shall run and not be weary, they shall walk and not faint" (Isaiah 40:31). Patience is a great virtue when walking with God.

Sin and Guilt

The subject of sin is well understood by almost everybody because the Bible says that all have sinned (Romans 3:23). To take it further, the Bible also says, "Whatever is not of faith is sin" (Romans 14:23), which includes prayers that are not said in faith or by faith. I am not going to discuss the broad spectrum of sin but only as it relates to prayer. Any form of unconfessed sin can hinder our prayers.

However, sin need not hinder us when we prayer because there is forgiveness in God. God has the power to forgive any sin. We must not allow the knowledge or consciousness of past or present sin to hinder us from praying effectively. If we retain any unconfessed sin it will definitely hinder our prayers.I have been asked many times, "Does forgiveness of sin abolish God's punishment for sin? Can God forgive sin but still punish the individual?" There are different schools of though on this subject. 1 John 1:9 tells us, "If we confess our sin He is faithful and just to forgive us our sin and to cleanse us from all unrighteousness." I have said before that our prayers are answered at the time and point of prayer. If a sin is confessed as soon as it is committed before God pronounces or metes out the punishment, it could eliminate the need for punishment.

However, if we continue to try to hide our sin from God and confess it after He has pronounced the punishment, His Word cannot return to Him void. It must accomplish its purpose (Isaiah 55:11). The reason Jesus came was to save us from the penalties of our sins, not just to keep us from going to hell, but to receive God's mercy while still here on the earth. God desires to extend mercy to all of His children rather than punishment. Let us read what God said through Ezekiel even in the Old Testament.

> *"Have I any pleasure at all that the wicked should die? Saith the Lord God: and not that he should return from His ways and live." Again, when a wicked man turns away from the wickedness which he committed, and does what is lawful and right, he preserves himself alive. Because he considers and turns away from all the transgressions which he committed, he shall surely live; he shall not die. Yet the house of Israel*

says, "The way of the Lord is not fair." O house of Israel, is it not My ways which are fair, and your ways which are not fair? Therefore I will judge you, O house of Israel, every one according to his ways," says the Lord God. "Repent, and turn from all your transgressions, so that iniquity will not be your ruin. Cast away from you all the transgressions which you have committed, and get yourselves a new heart and a new spirit. For why should you die, O house of Israel? For I have no pleasure in the death of one who dies," says the Lord God. "Therefore turn and live!"

(Ezekiel 18: 23, 25, 27-32)

God has no pleasure in punishing His children; and no earthly parent does either. Punishment is for correction if we fail to correct ourselves. God loves His children as no other parent can. His plans and thoughts for us are for good and not for punishment. That is what it is all about. When God forgives sin it is forgiven so you do not need to continue to live under the quilt of it.

In the case of David in 2 Samuel 12:9-16, David was hiding his sin with Bathsheba and did not confess it until Nathan the Prophet confronted him and pronounced God's punishment before He confessed it. The same was true for Saul the King of Israel. He failed to confess his sin until Samuel confronted him with it and pronounced the punishment before he confessed it. Let us learn to confess our faults before the devil takes it up to God to use against us.

You can confess your sins to God through the name of Jesus just like any other request. Jesus told us if we ask any thing in His Name He will do it. He promised to answer our prayers if we ask in faith. Everyone has the knowledge of the sin he or she committed or are committing. Sin is a polluter and when your heart is polluted by sin, your whole being (body, soul, and spirit) knows it. Sin is never hidden in our sub-consciousness no matter how much we want to suppress it. As sin is obvious to our conscience so it is to God. There is no point trying to hide it from God. He already knows. He was there when you committed that sin. Therefore, to make sure that sin does not hinder your prayer, confess it at once and have peace with God. And better still, forsake it.Part of the reason there is so much crime and wickedness in our society today is the guilt of unconfessed and unforgiven sins. So many of the sicknesses and diseases in our lives could be a result of unconfessed sins built up over the years which have compounded, and are now limiting, aggravating and inhibiting factors in our lives.When sin remains unconfessed and stays a long time in the system, it could merge with other sins of like nature, take on another spiritual and emotion nature or dimension and become more complex than either of the original sins. You might forget the original sins or lose the consciousness of them, but they are still retained until they are confessed individually or as a group. It is never late to confess a sin. God will forgive any time we confess. Forgiveness is His nature. It is His will for us. The point I want to make here is that unconfessed sin is dangerous. It is corrosive, it is toxic, and it is lethal. It can literally kill. Sin has its own power to kill. The Bible says in Romans 6: 23, "For the wages of sin is death, but the gift of God is eternal life in Christ Jesus our Lord James 1:15 says, "Then when lust has conceived it brings forth sin, and sin, when it is finished, brings forth death." Don't let it stay for another day once you feel the guilt of it. Confess your sin immediately until you receive the peace of forgiveness. Some sins are very subtle in nature, they are hard to recognize and get rid of. The reason is because they agree with our way of thinking. They justify our actions and blame others for what we have done or are still doing. Such sins as unbelief, unforgiveness, doubt, bitterness, hatred, jealousy, and lingering anger can sometimes be hard to detect. Living under guilt for a long time is a sin in its own because it is a form of unforgiveness of self.Living under guilt for a long time hinders prayer and impedes growth. Most other sins like fornication, adultery, murder, and stealing are very obvious and should be confessed or dealt with immediately or they will begin to hinder prayer. All unrighteousness is sin.Jesus came to destroy the works of the devil. The superior power in the superior name of Jesus can wipe away any sin in an instant. That is one of the reasons it is called the name above every other name. Not only does God forgive sin through the name of Jesus Christ, He also wipes it away forever so that there will be no remembrance of it again. "I, even I, am He who blots out your transgressions for My own sake; And I will not remember your sins" (Isaiah 43:25).In Psalm 103:10-12 it says, "He has not dealt with us according to our sins, nor punished us according to our iniquities. For as the heavens are high above the earth, so great is His mercy toward those who fear Him; As far as the east is from the west, So far has He removed our transgressions from us."Some people believe that God forgives sin but are not quite sure whether He forgets it or not. My belief is that He also forgets it. Jesus said,"Let it be to you according to your faith" (Matthew 9:29). In order to prevent sin from hindering our prayers, we should form the habit of confessing our sins when we sin or feel the guilt of them. Sin brings fear and self-condemnation. God may not hear us when we retain unconfessed sins. The heart is the dwelling place of God. He wants it to be clean and sacred. Consequently, obedience to the Word of God brings faith and favor from God. We should at all times be faith-minded, have a faith mentality, and not be fear-minded or live with a fear mentality.

Chapter 11

The Name Above All Names

There are many and compelling reasons why we should use the name of Jesus more regularly in our prayers, meditations, worship, battles against the forces of evil, confessions, and spiritual discussions.

The Manifested Christ

The name Jesus is the manifested Christ or Messiah. The name represents the presence and power of the risen Master. The name of Jesus is to the church today what His physical presence in the flesh was to the disciples. Jesus was with the disciples 24/7, that is, every hour and everyday of the week. He went nowhere without them except when He went to pray. He was their closest Friend, Companion, Master, Savior, Healer, Provider, Confidant, Mentor, and Lord. He was never out of their sight. He was the Bible or Scripture they read and heard. Jesus lived out the prophecies of the Bible before their very eyes. He was with them until His very last minute on earth. So the disciples got to know Him very, intimately. When Jesus rose from the dead, He continued to appear to them and they were with Him when He was taken up into heaven. Before

He died Jesus promised them that He would never leave them alone nor forsake them. He kept that promise in His life, death, and resurrection. "Let your conduct be without covetousness; be content with such things as you have. For He Himself has said, 'I will never leave you nor forsake you'" (Hebrews 13:5).

> *"And I will pray the Father, and He will give you another Helper, that He may abide with you for-ever—the Spirit of truth, whom the world cannot receive, because it neither sees Him nor knows Him; but you know Him, for He dwells with you and will be in you. I will not leave you orphans; I will come to you."*
>
> (John 14:16-18)

Jesus is still with us today in the power of His name. He is with us in the spirit of His name. He promised to walk with us in the power of His name and in the power of the Holy Ghost. He taught and instructed His disciples to use His name in everything they did, so they knew and used His name even in their own daily ministrations. "Then the seventy returned with joy, saying, 'Lord, even the demons are subject to us in Your name'"(Luke 10:17).Paul echoed the words of Jesus to the church at Colossae, "And whatever you do in word or deed, do all in the name of the Lord Jesus, giving thanks to God the Father through Him" (Colossians 3:19).From the time Jesus ascended, the disciples were using His name to do all things that their Lord and Master would have done had He been there physically. The name of Jesus never failed them just as the physical Jesus never failed them. It brought Peter out from the prison twice, healed sicknesses and disease, cast out demons, turned

Philip into a miracle worker who could travel in the spirit without a horse or chariot, rescued and delivered Paul many times from danger and death, and so much more. The name of Jesus can do the same now if we preach the gospel as the early disciples did. The name of Jesus is here with us, it is here to stay, so use it. It is given free of charge.

Prayer Empowerment

The name of Jesus was given to us to empower our prayer. It gives power, momentum, and the lift or boost our prayer requires to take off and reach the presence of the Father. It places our prayers right in the hands of Jesus and makes our prayer His prayer and our word His word. It empowers prayer because Jesus cannot see our prayers fail without seeing Himself as a failure also. Someone then asked, "Can there be wrong prayers? If so how can we claim that our prayers are His prayers?" There can be wrong prayers that may seem right in our own eyes. This is where the issue of motive comes in. If our motive is wrong then the prayer is wrong from God's perspective. When the children of God asked for a king in 1 Samuel 8:1-6, their request displeased God because it meant they had rejected Him as their King. Even though God answered their prayer and gave them a king, that was not His desire for them.

Jesus rebuked His disciples when they asked if they should pray and call down fire from heaven to consume a village that did not receive them (Luke 9:54-56). Any prayer that is not acceptable to God is a wrong prayer. Any prayer that is not according to the will of God is a wrong prayer. There is a tremendous energizing power in the name of Jesus and it is transferred to prayer when we pray in His name. Using the name of Jesus properly in prayer energizes you to pray more and pray long, because you know you will get what you are asking from God. It encourages you to live a godly life because you know you have a living relationship with Jesus through His name. It makes you hallow, honor, appreciate, and glorify Jesus more. The name of Jesus brings you closer to God in your word and deed. Jesus is in His name and in His word to defend and exalt it.Those who have learned the secret of using the name of Jesus are a terror to Satan and the kingdom of darkness. There is nothing else in this world that will empower your prayer more than the name of Jesus. It is the only name that Satan fears. It is the only name he does not want to hear or confront. Each time he tried to do battle with the name of Jesus, he was disgraced, humiliated or defeated. Therefore, if you want to keep the devil out of your life and property, learn to use the name of Jesus in an acceptable way.

Power Releaser

There is always a stupendous release of power anytime the name of Jesus is mentioned in spirit and truth. The kingdom of darkness knows it and fears that name. Every demon in the pit of hell has heard the name of Jesus. Whenever His name is mentioned correctly there is always a commotion and confusion in their midst. They fall over each other to find a place to bow or escape. For example, whenever the demon possessed encountered Jesus in His earthly ministry, they would bow and worship Him.

When he saw Jesus from afar, he ran and worshiped Him. And he cried out with a loud voice and said, "What have I to do with You, Jesus, Son of the Most

*High God? I implore You by God that You do not
torment me."*

(Mark 5:6-7)

*When he saw Jesus, he cried out, fell down before
Him, and with a loud voice said, "What have I to do
with You, Jesus, Son of the Most High God? I beg
You, do not torment me!"*

(Luke 8:28)

The name of Jesus will torment Satan and his host; that
is why we should not fear what the devil can do to us, the
believing ones. Similarly, Jesus said that Satan entered into
Judas, and presumably into those that came with him to
arrest Jesus in the garden of Gethsemane. Read what happened when He spoke His name to the belligerent crowd.

*Jesus therefore, knowing all things that would come
upon Him, went forward and said to them, "Whom
are you seeking?" They answered Him, "Jesus of
Nazareth." Jesus said to them, "I am He." And
Judas, who betrayed Him, also stood with them.
Now when He said to them, "I am He," they drew
back and fell to the ground."*

(John 18:4-6)

Even today this same phenomenon is still happening
in crusades and deliverance services all over the world.
It is obvious that there is a tremendous release of power
when the name of Jesus is mentioned properly, and when
it comes in contact with the forces of evil. The name of
Jesus is the greatest of all names, far surpassing any other
anywhere in the universe. We underrate the name as we
become too unnecessarily familiar with it, and so it appears

to have lost its power. No, it has not and it never will! The name of Jesus is the same yesterday, today, and forevermore, Hebrews 13:8. I believe that there is a "safety valve" that protects the power in the name from being abused or used for unnecessary and ungodly purposes. It cannot be turned off or removed, therefore, it appears as if it does not work. But for those who know Him, who come by faith, and praying in His will, there is no restriction to the power in the name of Jesus. In Jeremiah 29:13 God said, "And you will seek Me and find Me, when you search for Me with all your heart." The power in the name of Jesus is readily available all the time to all those who believe in Him out of a pure heart. Jesus is full of love and compassion and wants to share His love and power with us all. He will never drive anyone away who comes to Him with a believing heart (John 6:37). Psalm 84:11 says, "For the Lord God is a sun and shield; the Lord will give grace and glory; No good thing will He withhold from those who walk uprightly."

Power for Salvation

Salvation through Jesus Christ is a simple but spiritual process by which a sinner receives pardon for sin and the hope of eternal life. It is an all inclusive redemptive work: grace, forgiveness, justification, sanctification, glorification, and reconciliation peace and much more. Salvation is the only means by which man can be saved from the curse of the law and from Adamic curses. Acts 4:12 states, "Neither is there salvation in any other, for there is no other name under heaven given among men by which we must be saved." Salvation is for the restoration of relationship with our Holy and Righteous God. Salvation brings man into a living, loving, and active relationship with the risen

Jesus as if He is physically present. However, salvation is not as cheap as it seem. It cost Jesus shame, disgrace, rejection, agony, and ultimately His life. It cost God the life of His only beloved Son. It took generations upon generations in planning and preparation. Salvation opens the door for direct access into the presence of God to anyone who believes in Jesus Christ. What only Moses and few other prophets were able to accomplish, not by their own strength, is now available to all. It didn't come cheap and it is still not cheap. Salvation is a complete transformation, restoration, and recreation of the human spirit. It is being born again of the human spirit, in order for man to have the ability to interact directly with his Creator. Salvation produces eternal life in the heart of the believer. In John 3:3-5, Jesus explained this to a Jewish leader, Nicodemus.

Jesus answered and said to him, "Most assuredly, I say to you, unless one is born again, he cannot see the kingdom of God." Nicodemus said to Him, "How can a man be born when he is old? Can he enter a second time into his mother's womb and be born?" Jesus answered, "Most assuredly, I say to you, unless one is born of water and the Spirit, he cannot enter the kingdom of God."

It takes power to be "born again" just as it takes power to be born into this world the first time. John 1:12 says, "But as many as received Him, to them gave He power to become the sons of God, even to them that believe on His name." Consider the process a pregnant woman must go through during the final moments before the birth of her child. The midwife or doctor instructs the woman to push with all her power. When she does so, a child is born into this world. If she were to lose strength, both their lives would be in jeopardy. It also takes the power of God to be born into the kingdom of God. It took the power of God to raise Jesus from the dead after three days in the grave. Salvation is not easy and certainly not cheap. After salvation, a child of God also requires the power of the Holy Ghost to "work out, cultivate, carry out the goal, and fully complete your own salvation with reverence and awe" (Philippians 2:12 AMP) and daily walk with Jesus. Paul said in Romans 1:16, "For I am not ashamed of the gospel of Christ, for it is the power of God unto salvation to everyone who believes." Salvation comes through the power of the gospel of Christ. The gospel is all about the ministry of Jesus Christ, His death, and His resurrection. You cannot be saved or born again without the power in the name of Jesus. Salvation is a complete package which includes, but is not limited to the gifts of: faith, eternal life, healings, gifts of the Holy Spirit, deliverance, wholeness, wellness, peace, love, joy, and prosperity. All that we desire such as long life, health, money, and solutions to life's problems are included in the total package and are available through the name of Jesus Christ to any one who believes.

Holy Ghost Releaser

Jesus is the name that releases the power and anointing of the Holy Ghost. It is He who baptizes with the Holy Ghost. On the day of Pentecost, Jesus fulfilled the promise He made to the disciples shortly before He ascended into heaven. He said to them, "Behold, I (will) send the Promise of My Father upon you; but tarry in the city of Jerusalem until you are endued with power from on high" (Luke 24:49).As they gathered together to pray and fellowship, suddenly Jesus visited them with the most powerful out-pouring of the Holy Ghost ever recorded in history. They saw what appeared as tongues of fire coming down on each of them. As it rested on their heads, they suddenly began to speak in new languages to the amazement of all those who witnessed that strange phenomenon. Peter quickly under-stood what was happening and allayed the fears, confusion, and disbelieve of those who had gathered. He told them that what they were witnessing had been prophesied by the prophet Joel, and enjoined them to be part of it by repenting and receiving the gift of the Holy Ghost. He told them that the baptism of the Holy Ghost was equally for them and their children, both far and near, and for as many as would answer God's call for repentance unto salvation. From that day until now, God has been pouring out the gift and bap-tizing believers with the Holy Ghost. It is only through the name of Jesus that you can receive this wonderful gift of speaking in new tongues. If you really believe it, desire it with all of your heart, and call on the name of Jesus out of a sincere heart, you will receive it.

> *Then Peter said to them, "Repent, and let every one of you be baptized in the name of Jesus Christ for the remission of sins; and you shall receive the gift of the Holy Spirit. For the promise is to you and to your children, and to all who are afar off, as many as the Lord our God will call."*

(Acts 2:38-39).

The key words are **repent and believe**. People some-times need the help of a pastor or an evangelist to manifest the gift of speaking in tongues. If you do, please contact your local pastor or contact me directly.

Now when the apostles who were at Jerusalem heard that Samaria had received the word of God, they sent Peter and John to them, who, when they had come down, prayed for them that they might receive the Holy Spirit. For as yet He had fallen upon none of them. They had only been baptized in the name of the Lord Jesus. Then they laid hands on them, and they received the Holy Spirit.

(Acts 8:12)

While Peter was still speaking these words, the Holy Spirit fell upon all those who heard the word; And those of the circumcision who believed were astonished, as many as came with Peter, because the gift of the Holy Spirit had been poured out on the Gentiles also.

(Acts 10:44-45)

He said to them, "Did you receive the Holy Spirit when you believed?" So they said to him, "We have not so much as heard whether there is a Holy Spirit." And he said to them, "Into what then were you baptized?" So they said, "Into John's baptism." Then Paul said, "John indeed baptized with a baptism of repentance, saying to the people that they should believe on Him who would come after him, that is, on Christ Jesus." When they heard this, they were baptized in the name of the Lord Jesus. And when Paul had laid hands on them, the Holy Spirit came upon them, and they spoke with tongues and prophesied.

(Acts 19:2, 5-6)

Once when I was pastoring a church in Nigeria, a deacon from a popular Pentecostal church came to me one Sunday morning before service.

He said, "Pastor, I have been praying for the baptism of the Holy Ghost for many years but have not been successful, can you help me?"

Of course, I said yes and then I asked him if he was ready.

He said, "With all my heart."As I laid my hand on him and prayed with him in the name of Jesus, he immediately received the Holy Ghost and started speaking in tongues. Psalm 81:10 says, "Open your mouth wide and I will fill it." We witnessed many other such releases of the baptism of the Spirit during our ministrations.

Chapter 12

Jesus Will Never Leave You

For He Himself has said, "I will never leave you nor forsake you." So we may boldly say: "The Lord is my helper; I will not fear."

(Hebrews 13:5-6 NKJV)

The Rod of Moses

To the believer, the name of Jesus is like the rod of Moses. The rod of Moses symbolized the power of God with Him and the children of Israel. The difference is that the rod was a physical stick that could be seen, touched, and felt. But the name of Jesus is a spiritual power. You can never see, feel or touch it; nevertheless it is as potent, even more powerful, and more effective than the rod of Moses. What the name of Jesus is in the mouth of the believers today is what the rod was in the hand of Moses then. Jesus was the "Angel" that led the children of Israel through the wilderness experience.Moses used that rod to do miracles and some incredible things. The apostles of Jesus, believers down through the millennia, and still today the power of the name of Jesus accomplishes amazing things. The name of Jesus in our mouth is closer to us than the rod of Moses in this great leader's hand. The world does not yet understand all that the name of Jesus means to the heart of the Father. Christians still do not know what they are carrying in their mouth and in their heart. Salvation is all inclusive and is available to all.

> *"The word is near you, in your mouth and in your heart" (that is, the word of faith which we preach): that if you confess with your mouth the Lord Jesus and believe in your heart that God has raised Him from the dead, you will be saved. For with the heart one believes unto righteousness, and with the mouth confession is made unto salvation."*
>
> (Romans 10:8-10)

It is no surprise that Moses did not know that the shepherd's stick that he took from the brushes was a mighty and terrible weapon when presented to God. In the same vein, we do not yet understand the power of this simple, five-letter word, J-E-S-U-S, until we present our mouth to God for sanctification and use. Man is limited in the knowledge of who he is and what he has until he presents himself to God for empowerment. Believers need to begin to yield their hearts to God because Jesus said, "Out of the resources (abundance) of the heart the mouth speaks." What comes out of our mouth reflects what we have stored in our heart. If the name of Jesus is honored in our heart it will come out of our mouth. If fear, doubt, and unbelief are enthroned in our heart it will also manifest in our words.

Child of God, what is in your heart? Is it faith in the name of Jesus or fear and unbelief? This question is for us all to answer.Moses used the rod of God in his hand to bring glory to God. May we also use the power in the name of Jesus in our Hearts and in our mouths to bring greater glory to the name of Jesus. The Apostle Paul said, "That I may know Him and the power of His resurrection" (Philippians 3:10).

Ever Present Companion

The name of Jesus is an ever present companion. This is perhaps the most important reason why you should allow the name of Jesus to abide in you as a very vital necessity. Colossian 3:16 says, "Let the word of Christ dwell in you richly in all wisdom, teaching and admonishing one another in psalms and hymns and spiritual songs, singing with grace in your hearts to the Lord." You could also add the word, Jesus and say: "Let the name of Jesus Christ dwell in you richly" because it can and will enrich every aspect of your life. The name of Jesus does more good than any medicine. Proverbs 17: 22 says, "A merry heart does good, like medicine, but a broken spirit dries the bones."It can bring merriness and joy unspeakable into your heart. Jesus is with you all day and all night. His name goes before, behind, above, beneath, beside, and all around you. The name of Jesus lives in your heart and in every tissue of your being; in as much room as you give it by faith. It is your closest ally. It will go with you where nothing else and no one else will go. If He lives in the fiber of your tissues He will heal your body even to your bone marrow, and every delicate part that the surgeon's knife cannot reach.Jesus will guide you, teach you, instruct you, defend you, protect, promote, and project you by the spirit of His name. Jesus never fails. Heaven and earth may pass away, but Jesus will never fail you if you put your total trust in Him. When you commit yourself and your ways completely, absolutely, and unconditionally to His will, He will carry you on eagle's wings.

Commit your way to the Lord, Trust also in Him, and He shall bring it to pass. He shall bring forth your righteousness as the light, and your justice as the noonday. Rest in the Lord, and wait patiently for Him; Do not fret because of him who prospers in his way, Because of the man who brings wicked schemes to pass.

(Psalm 37:5-6)

Jesus is God and He is in the spirit of His name. As we have seen, all power in heaven, on earth, and underneath the earth is vested in that name. The omnipresence, the omnipotence, and the omniscience of the Godhead are all vested in that name. Therefore, you can never be alone working with that name. He is and will ever be your very present companion and helper. Jesus is in His name. He is not different from His name. He is not a man and He cannot lie. He cannot deceive and He cannot fail. Proverbs 3:5 says, "Trust in the Lord with all your heart, and lean not on your own understanding; in all your ways acknowledge Him, and He shall direct your paths." God has come down to be with humanity. Emmanuel is with us in the spirit of His name. His name not only represents Him, His name is Jesus the Lord.

Ambassadorial Powers

The ultimate purpose for which Jesus gave us His name is so that we can take His place here on earth and do the work that needs to be done here. He wants us to use His name to carry out His purposes in this world, represent Him physically among men, and have our needs and petitions met while doing His work. He in turn will represent us in heaven before the Father as our High Priest and intercessor. An Ambassador is the highest diplomatic representative appointed by a country to represent it in another country. We are citizens of heaven. We have been given the power to represent Christ here on earth. Jesus Himself expressly authorized us to use His name to represent Him as His disciples and His ambassadors. There is therefore no reason to be ashamed, afraid or doubtful. He did not put any restrictions on the use of that name, although I have had people tell me they didn't want to bother God too much. God is impressed and pleased when we put His name to genuine and appropriate use. After all, it is for that purpose Jesus gave us the name in the first place. Jesus wants to work in partnership with us in propagating the Kingdom of God on earth in order to hasten His return. Christ is eager to come back to His own—the church. He did not want the world to forget about Him after He was gone, therefore, He gave us His name as a helper, a companion, and a constant reminder that He is coming back again. Just as He gave us the Holy Communion as a constant reminder of His death and resurrection, so He gave us His name to remind us that He is coming again.I believe that God might have us account for what we did with power we were given in His name. If Jesus would ask us what we did with this valuable gift, what would your response be? There is power; there is superior authority in the name of Jesus. Do not treat it with levity. It is worth more than the whole world to God.

Miracle Producer

The life and ministry of Jesus were dominated by healings, miracles, signs, wonders, and blessings. So it was also in the lives of the early apostles and disciples. Jesus performed more than 34 recorded miracles during His ministry. According to John the beloved apostle, " Miracles are an important part of the church life and ministry. As goes the leader so goes the followership. We are followers of Jesus Christ. Jesus said, "Most assuredly, I say to you, he who believes in Me, the works that I do he will do also; and greater works than these he will do, because I go to My Father" (John 14:12). The New International Version renders John 14:12, "I tell you the truth, anyone who has faith in me will do what I have been doing. He will do even greater things than these, because I am going to the Father."The name of Jesus is the miracle producer, not our own power. The name works with our own faith to produce the required or desired miracles. Seeing miracles everyday of your life, whether they are great or small, proves your faith in the name of Jesus. It is an indication that you are living an active Christian life. It means also that you are using the name appropriately.On the other hand, a protracted lack of miracles in the life of a Christian believer could indicate a dwindling faith in the power of that name or it could mean that your zeal for the things of God is turning cold. It could also mean that you may not be a believer at all. In the two scriptural renditions above, Jesus says "anyone who has faith or believes in Me shall…" indicating the work and miracles He did are only possible to those who believe and have faith in Him.

And these signs will accompany those who believe: In my name they will drive out demons; they will speak in new tongues; they will pick up snakes with their hands; and when they drink deadly poison, it will not hurt them at all; they will place their hands on sick people, and they will get well.

(Mark 16:17)

Miracles in the life of a believer are a sure sign of his abiding faith in the name of the Son of God. They do no always have to be earth shaking miracles. They could be as simple as praying and being healed of a fever. After all, Jesus healed Peter's mother-in-law of a fever. However, seeing or working miracles does not make one superior or better than any other person. They only attest to the fact that you have faith in Jesus Christ.Actually no miracle is small by any means. Miracles are direct interventions of the divine in the lives and activities of men. Miracles testify that Jesus is alive and active in us and in the world. Friend, when did you last see or witness a miracle in your life? May God give you new miracles everyday for the remainder of your life.

Name Above Every Name

*Wherefore God also hath highly exalted him, and **given him a name which is above every name**: That at the name of Jesus every knee should bow, of things in heaven, and things in earth, and things under the earth; And that every tongue should confess that Jesus Christ is Lord, to the glory of God the Father.*

(Philippians 2:9-11)

126

And his name shall be called Wonderful, Counselor, Mighty God, Everlasting Father, Prince of Peace.
(Isaiah 9:6-7)

There has never been and will never be any other name with such titles and exaltations as the name of Jesus Christ. God the Father conferred on Jesus the greatest name in the universe, which represents His position in the Godhead, and His achievements in the plan of salvation. The name of Jesus is and will be the most trusted and honored on the earth.

It has the power to save, heal, deliver, bless, help, and perform miracles. It is a name recognized in heaven and on earth. It is the only name through which mortal men can tap the divine power of God for use here on earth. It is loaded with power and authority. In the name of Jesus impossible situations are made possible. Through it, and only through it, prayers receive answers. The reason you should use the name of Jesus is because it is the All-Sufficient, Everlasting and Ever-Living name that gives you hope, freedom, inspired faith, and confidence in the face of insurmountable odds.

It Is a Good Name

The name of Jesus is a good name. It is a sweet name. It is honorable and trustworthy. It is an excellent name. Proverbs 22:1 says, "A good name is more desirable than great riches; to be esteemed is better than silver or gold."Another translation renders it this way"A good name is rather to be chosen than great riches, and loving favor rather than silver and gold" (AMP).If you have an opportunity to choose between the name of Jesus and money, choose the name first because in it is everything else. The name of the Lord Jesus is not only good, but most excellent. This is because of the excellent things He has done and is still doing in the world and in people's lives today. David said,"O Lord, our Lord, How excellent is Your name in all the earth, Who have set Your glory above the heavens. When I consider Your heavens, the work of Your fingers, The moon and the stars, which You have ordained" (Psalm 8:1, 3).Everybody loves a good name. Jesus is that good name. It is not an ordinary name. It is not the name of a great politician. It is the name of God Himself. It is the name that moves mountains in people's lives. The scripture says, "In that name shall the gentiles (non-Jews) trust" (Matthew 12:21). That name is capable of changing your life and your situation if you trust in it and wait patiently. People like to associate with individuals who have good names and good reputation, but the name of Jesus has no equal or comparison. It is a supernatural name like no other. You should believe in and use the name of Jesus because it is a good name and the Most Excellent name in the entire universe. Oh how sweet and how excellent the name of Jesus sounds.

There is no one who has come close to Jesus and does not have at least a song, a story, an experience or a testimony to tell about His love, grace, kindness, peace of mind, forgiveness of sin, and joy in the Holy Ghost. Others have spoken of the friendship, favors, healings, miracles, deliverances, and other blessings they have received through His name.

And what more shall I say? I do not have time to tell about Gideon, Barak, Samson, Jephthah, David,

Samuel and the prophets, who through faith con-
quered kingdoms, administered justice, and gained
what was promised; who shut the mouths of lions,
quenched the fury of the flames, and escaped the
edge of the sword; whose weakness was turned to
strength; and who became powerful in battle and
routed foreign armies.

Women received back their dead raised to life
again. Others were tortured and refused to be
released, so that they might gain a better resur-
rection. Some faced jeers and flogging, while still
others were chained and put in prison. They were
stoned; they were sawed in two; they were put to
death by the sword."

(Hebrews 11:32-38)

There are many compelling reasons and testimonies
other than these few, both in the Scriptures and in the world
around us. This should make us want to know and use the
name of Jesus in our daily fight of faith. My prayer is the
same as Paul's in Ephesians 1:17-22.

"That the God of our Lord Jesus Christ, the Father
of glory, may give to you the spirit of wisdom and
revelation in the knowledge of Him, the eyes of your
understanding being enlightened; that you may know
what is the hope of His calling, what are the riches of
the glory of His inheritance in the saints, and what
is the exceeding greatness of His power toward us
who believe, according to the working of His mighty
power which He worked in Christ when He raised
Him from the dead and seated Him at His right hand
in the heavenly places, far above all principality and

power and might and dominion, and every name that is named, not only in this age but also in that which is to come. And He put all things under His feet, and gave Him to be head over all things to the church."

Chapter 13

Powerful Promises and Quotations

1. "But you shall receive power when the Holy Spirit has come upon you; and you shall be witnesses to Me in Jerusalem, and in all Judea and Samaria, and to the end of the earth." (Acts 1: 8)

2. Then Peter said, "Silver and gold I do not have, but what I do have I give you: In the name of Jesus Christ of Nazareth, rise up and walk." (Acts 3:6)

3. And His name, through faith in His name, has made this man strong, whom you see and know. Yes, the faith which comes through Him has given him this perfect soundness in the presence of you all. (Acts 3:16)

4. Neither is there salvation in any other, for there is no other name under heaven given among men by which we must be saved." (Acts 4:12)

5. "Behold, I send the Promise of My Father upon you; but tarry in the city of Jerusalem until you are endued with power from on high." (Luke 24:49)

6. Then Peter said to them, "Repent, and let every one of you be baptized in the name of Jesus Christ for the remission of sins; and you shall receive the gift of the Holy Spirit. For the promise is to you and to your children, and to all who are afar off, as many as the Lord our God will call." (Acts 2:38-39)

7. For where two or three are gathered together in My name, I am there in the midst of them." (Matthew 18:20)

8. And in His name Gentiles will trust. (Matthew 12:21)

9. "And she will bring forth a Son, and you shall call His name Jesus, for He will save His people from their sins." (Matthew 1:21)

10. Therefore the Lord Himself will give you a sign: Behold, the virgin shall conceive and bear a Son, and shall call His name Immanuel. (Isaiah 7:14)

11. "And you will be hated by all for My name's sake. But he who endures to the end will be saved." (Matthew 10:22)

12. "… and lo, I am with you always, even to the end of the age." (Matthew 28: 20)

13. "For assuredly, I say to you, whoever says to this mountain, 'Be removed and be cast into the sea,' and

does not doubt in his heart, but believes that those things he says will be done, he will have whatever he says. Therefore I say to you, whatever things you ask when you pray, believe that you receive them, and you will have them. (Mark 11:23-24)

14. "And these signs will follow those who believe: In My name they will cast out demons; they will speak with new tongues; they will take up serpents; and if they drink anything deadly, it will by no means hurt them; they will lay hands on the sick, and they will recover." (Mark 16:17-18)

15. "But as many as received Him, to them He gave the right to become children of God, to those who believe in His name." (John 1:12)

16. "Jesus answered and said to him, 'Most assuredly, I say to you, unless one is born again, he cannot see the kingdom of God'." (John 3:3)

17. "For God so loved the world that He gave His only begotten Son, that whoever believes in Him should not perish but have everlasting life." (John 3:16)

18. "…that whoever believes in Him should not perish but have eternal life." (John 3:15)

19. "He who believes in Him is not condemned; but he who does not believe is condemned already, because he has not believed in the name of the only begotten Son of God." (John 3:18)

20. "Most assuredly, I say to you, he who hears My word and believes in Him who sent Me has everlasting life, and shall not come into judgment, but has passed from death into life." (John 5:24)

21. "Most assuredly, I say to you, the hour is coming, and now is, when the dead will hear the voice of the Son of God; and those who hear will live." (John 5:25)

22. "All that the Father gives Me will come to Me, and the one who comes to Me I will by no means cast out." (John 6:37)

23. "Most assuredly, I say to you, he who believes in Me has everlasting life. I am the bread of life." (John 6:47-48)

24. "Then Jesus said to them, 'Most assuredly, I say to you, unless you eat the flesh of the Son of Man and drink His blood, you have no life in you'." (John 6:53)

25. "On the last day, that great day of the feast, Jesus stood and cried out, saying, 'If anyone thirsts, let him come to Me and drink. He who believes in Me, as the Scripture has said, out of his heart will flow rivers of living water'." (John 7:37-38)

26. "And Jesus said to her, 'Neither do I condemn you; go and sin no more'." (John 8:11)

27. "Then Jesus spoke to them again, saying, 'I am the light of the world. He who follows Me shall not walk in darkness, but have the light of life'." (John 8:12)

28. "And you shall know the truth, and the truth shall make you free." (John 8:32)

29. "Therefore if the Son makes you free, you shall be free indeed." (John 8:36)

30. "The thief does not come except to steal, and to kill, and to destroy. I have come that they may have life, and that they may have it more abundantly." (John 10:10)

31. "And I give them eternal life, and they shall never perish; neither shall anyone snatch them out of My hand." (John 10:28)

32. "…and the Scripture cannot be broken." (John 10:35)

33. "Jesus said to her, 'I am the resurrection and the life. He who believes in Me, though he may die, he shall live'." (John 11:25)

34. "And I, if I am lifted up from the earth, will draw all peoples to Myself." (John 12:32)

35. "A new commandment I give to you, that you love one another; as I have loved you, that you also love one another." (John 13:14)

36. "Let not your heart be troubled; you believe in God, believe also in Me. In My Father's house are many mansions; if it were not so, I would have told you. I go to prepare a place for you. And if I go and prepare a place for you, I will come again and receive you

to Myself; that where I am, there you may be also."
(John14:1-3)

37. "Jesus said to him, 'I am the way, the truth, and the life. No one comes to the Father except through Me'." (John14:6)

38. "Most assuredly, I say to you, he who believes in Me, the works that I do he will do also; and greater works than these he will do, because I go to My Father." (John 14:12)

39. "And whatever you ask in My name, that I will do, that the Father may be glorified in the Son. If you ask anything in My name, I will do it. If you love Me, keep My commandments." (John 14: 13-15)

40. "And I will pray the Father, and He will give you another Helper, that He may abide with you forever." (John 14:16)

41. "I will not leave you orphans; I will come to you." (John 14:18)

42. "Peace I leave with you, My peace I give to you; not as the world gives do I give to you. Let not your heart be troubled, neither let it be afraid." (John 14:27)

43. "You are already clean because of the word which I have spoken to you." (John 15:3)

44. "I am the vine, you are the branches. He who abides in Me, and I in him, bears much fruit; for without Me you can do nothing." (John 15:5)

45. "If you abide in Me, and My words abide in you, you will ask what you desire, and it shall be done for you." (John 15:7)

46. "No longer do I call you servants, for a servant does not know what his master is doing; but I have called you friends, for all things that I heard from My Father I have made known to you." (John 15:15)

47. "You did not choose Me, but I chose you and appointed you that you should go and bear fruit, and that your fruit should remain, that whatever you ask the Father in My name He may give you." (John 15:16)

48. "I will see you again and your heart will rejoice, and your joy no one will take from you." (John 16:22)

49. "And in that day you will ask Me nothing. Most assuredly, I say to you, whatever you ask the Father in My name He will give you." (John 16:23)

50. "Until now you have asked nothing in My name. Ask, and you will receive, that your joy may be full." (John 16:24)

51. "These things I have spoken to you, that in Me you may have peace. In the world you will have tribulation; but be of good cheer, I have overcome the world." (John 16:33)

52. "I am the Alpha and the Omega, the Beginning and the End," says the Lord, "who is and who was and who is to come, the Almighty." (Revelation 1:8)

53. "I am Alpha and Omega, the First and Last..." (Revelation 1:11)

54. "I am He who lives, and was dead, and behold, I am alive forevermore. Amen. And I have the keys of Hades and of Death." (Revelation 1:18)

55. "He who has an ear, let him hear what the Spirit says to the churches. He who overcomes shall not be hurt by the second death." (Revelation 2:11)

56. "Behold, I stand at the door and knock. If anyone hears My voice and opens the door, I will come in to him and dine with him, and he with Me." (Revelation 3:20)

57. "And behold, I am coming quickly, and My reward is with Me, to give to every one according to his work. I am the Alpha and the Omega, the Beginning and the End, the First and the Last." (Revelation 22:12-13)

Miracles of Jesus

1. Turning water into wine John 2:1
2. Healing of official's son John 4:46-54
3. Healing of a man with unclean spirit Mark 1:23
4. Healing of Peter's mother-in-law Matt 8:14, Mark 1:29, Luke 4:38
5. Healing the sick at sun set Matt 8:16, Mark 1:32
6. Peter catching a large number of fish Luke 5:4

7. Healing a leper Matt 8:2, Mark 1:40, Luke 5:12
8. Healing the centurion's servant Matt 8:5, Luke 7:1
9. Healing a man with paralysis Matt 9:2, Mark 2:3 Luke 5:18
10. Healing the man with withered hand Matt 12:10, Mark 3:1, Luke 6:6
11. Raising a widow's son at Nain Luke 7:11
12. Calming the storm Matt 8:23, Mark 4:37, Luke 8:22
13. Healing a demon-possessed man at Garasene Luke 8:26-33
14. Healing a woman with the issue of blood Matt 9:20, Mark 5:25, Luke 8:43 Matt .
15. Raising of Jairus' daughter Matt:9:18, Mark 5:22, Luke 8:41
16. Healing the two blind men Matt 20:29
17. Healing a dumb man possessed by a demon Matt 9:32
18. Healing the man crippled for 38 years John 5:1
19. Feeding of the 5000 Matt. 14:15, Mark 6:35, Luke 9:12, John 6:6
20. Jesus walking on the water Matt 14:25, Mark 6: 48
21. Healing of many sick people in Gennesaret Matt 14:35
22. Healing the Syrophenician girl Matt 15:21, Mark 7:24
23. Healing a deaf and dumb man Mark 7:31
24. Feeding the 4000 men Matt 15:32, Mark 8:1
25. Healing the blind man in Bethsaida Mark 8:22
26. Healing the that was man born blind John 9:1
27. Healing the boy possessed by a demon Mark 9:17
28. Catching of a fish with a coin in its mouth Matt. 17:24

29. Healing a blind and dumb man who was possessed Matt 12:22
30. Healing a woman with a spirit of infirmity Luke 13:11
31. Healing the man with dropsy Luke 14:1
32. Healing the ten leper Luke 17:1133.
    Raising Lazarus from the dead John 11:1-44 34.
    Healing blind Bartimaeus Matt. 20:29, Mark 10: 46, Luke 18:35
35. The withered fig tree Matt. 21:18, Mark 11:12,
36. Healing of Malchus ear Luke 22: 51
37. The resurrection of Christ Matt. 28:1, Mark 16:1, Luke 24:1, John 20:1
38. Catching of the 153 fish John 21:11
39. The ascension of Jesus Christ Acts 1:9
40. Other Healings Matt. 4: 23

Other Books by the author:

The Amazing Power of Grace

♕

CPSIA information can be obtained at www.ICGtesting.com
Printed in the USA
LVOW130553210213

320992LV00002B/19/P

9 781625 090621